Everyone faces adver[sity] these difficulties tha[t] Duduit shares how s[ome] life's challenges, and [ ] as our guide. Another winner from a gifted author and encourager.

—Bruce A. Stewart, award-winning author of
Sing Me Something Happy

In today's world, the word "hero" has lost its luster and impact. Young people and sports fans in general are told that statistics and performance on the field is what makes an athlete "hero" material. In *First Down Devotions II*, Del Duduit shows us that an athlete's performance and character off the field has far more impact than any of their on-the-field exploits. A hero is made by their character, their conviction, and their caring; not who media pundits tell us our heroes should be. *First Down Devotions II* gives sports fans of all ages examples of extraordinary athletes who shine their brightest through the way they live their lives of faith and caring for their fellow man. With each short story, I found myself considering various traits and actions that I am encouraged to add to my life.

—J. D. Wininger, author

Del leads the reader to the greatest championship in *First Down Devotions II*—being a champion for Christ. Each devotion gives the reader a look at their heroes from the field behind the curtain, highlighting their faith even more than their play on the field. As one of the greatest sportswriters of our time, Del tells the story and adds applicable truths to move you from the sidelines to the end zone in your faith. Every football fan needs a copy of *First Down Devotions II* as it ensures your life in Christ is a Hall-of-Fame caliber walk with Christ.

—Andy Clapp, pastor and author of *Midnight, Christmas Eve*

In *First Down Devotions II*, respected author and journalist Del Duduit has developed a resource that provides biblical insight (which always withstands the test of time) and applicable truths that will benefit any reader spiritually.

—Robert Brooks, Athletes in Action Pro Ministry, NFL Chaplain

Other books in the Stars of the Faith Series

Dugout Devotions: Inspirational Hits from MLB's Best
Dugout Devotions II: More Inspirational Hits from MLB's Best
First Down Devotions: Inspiration from the NFL's Best
Auburn Believer: 40 Days of Devotions for the Tiger Faithful
Bama Believer: 40 Days of Devotions for the Roll Tide Faithful

FIRST DOWN
DEVOTIONS II

MORE INSPIRATION FROM NFL'S BEST

DEL DUDUIT

IRON STREAM
BOOKS
An imprint of Iron Stream Media
Birmingham, Alabama

Iron Stream Books
100 Missionary Ridge
Birmingham, AL 35242
IronStreamMedia.com
Iron Stream Books is an imprint of Iron Stream Media

Published in association with Cyle Young of the Hartline Literary Agency, LLC.

Library of Congress Control Number: 2021937415

ISBN: 978-1-56309-374-6 (paperback)
ISBN: 978-1-56309-378-4 (ebook)

Printed in the United States of America
1 2 3 4 5—25 24 23 22 21

This book is dedicated to my grandson, Joel.

Your unconditional love for me is amazing. I hope that never changes.

The way you said "papaw" when you were two years old always melted my heart.

You taught me to be young again and how to make spending time with people you love a priority. The most precious memories I have when this book was written was sharing ice cream on Friday afternoons with you, your grandmother, and your big sister at Dairy Queen.

Those memories will never leave me.

You won't recall this, but I adored it when you said, "Oh wow!" when you spotted trees while we walked down the street and how you imitated "Ralph" with the words "Holy cow!"

No matter what unexpected turns life may take, always know you are dear and special to me. I hope to make you proud of me, the same way I light up when I talk about you to anyone who will listen.

And one day, I hope this little book I wrote will have a resting place somewhere in your heart.

Be the best example of godly man and brother to your sister. Honor your parents and always be kind. But most of all never lose the desire to serve God.

I love you so much.

Papaw

CONTENTS

The following people played a significant role in the completion of this book, and I want to thank them personally.

My wife, Angie, for being the initial editor and supporting me through this process.

My agent, Cyle Young, for believe in me and assisting in making this a reality.

NFL Chaplain Robert Brooks for writing the foreword.

The *Portsmouth Daily Times* and their assistance with media credentials.

The following for contributing chapters in this book:

1. Beckie Lindsey
2. Ryan Farr
3. Cyle Young
4. Scott McCausey
5. Michelle Medlock Adams

John Herring and Ramona Richards at Iron Stream Media and New Hope Publishers for their faith in me.

Susan Cornell for her edits and making this book better.

And many thanks, as always, to God for His forgiveness and for giving me this wonderful opportunity.

FOREWORD

People of faith often read a devotion on a daily basis to learn, grow, and strengthen their foundation of faith. If you are one of these people, you will find yourself coming back to this devotional again and again.

In *First Down Devotions II*, respected author and journalist Del Duduit has developed a resource that provides biblical insight (which always withstands the test of time) and applicable truths that will benefit any reader spiritually.

He effectively draws the reader in through his connective writing style which enables you to transfer the concept from the page into your life with ease. You will celebrate the up-close look into the faith-filled lives of each individual contributor and be encouraged with how the Bible plays a tremendous role in their lives on and off the field.

Resources that contribute to the spiritual nourishment of the players, coaches, and administration within the NFL, help provide valuable touchpoints between a chaplain and the organizations they serve.

I have no doubt that this book of devotions will be a touchdown in the locker room and at home.

Robert Brooks
Athletes in Action Pro Ministry
NFL Chaplain

DAY 1
YOU BE THE INFLUENCE

Case Keenum
Quarterback
Cleveland Browns

By Del Duduit

Whoever walks with the wise becomes wise, but the companion of fools will suffer harm.

—Proverbs 13:20

During Case Keenum's time playing in the NFL, he's had the opportunity to build solid friendships with his teammates on different squads, and he enjoys the potential to have a positive influence in the locker room.

Case learned the significance of letting his light shine to others when he was a young man involved with the Fellowship of Christian Athletes.

The FCA challenges coaches and athletes at all levels to use their platforms to share the power of Jesus Christ with everyone. The organization serves local communities around the globe and inspires others to change the world with the gospel.

"It's been a big part of my life," Case said. "I grew up in the FCA family—it's in my blood so to speak."

His father was a director in West Texas, his wife was a coordinator in Houston, and his sister was a camp director in the Lone Star State as well.

"We have all stuffed envelopes and volunteered at different events," he said. "I grew up around athletes, especially Christian athletes, and they had an impact on me. I wanted to be like them in many ways."

He wanted to throw the football like them and talk like they did.

"I wanted to be like them in every way when I was young," he added. "It was the Christian athlete that really hit a cord with me. I found it was Christ in their life that they were shining for, and that's what I wanted to be like."

This inspiration is why Case invited Christ into his life when he was in the second grade. He was eager to learn from the right role models.

"That was the best decision I ever made," he said. "All of the people I admired and wanted to be like were all Christian athletes."

Hear, O sons, a father's instruction, and be attentive, that you may gain insight.

—Proverbs 4:1

In the Huddle

Who do you admire? Are the people you look up to in life good moral citizens? Do they do the right thing? Do you remember pretending to be like your favorite athletes when you were young? You probably picked up on their every action and tried to imitate them. Did they demonstrate positive character? On the other hand, who admires you? Who looks up to you and why? If you have children, they watch every step you take and hear every word you speak. Do you want them to be like you? Are there things you do that you don't want them to emulate?

Cross the Goal Line

You have the chance to make a difference in the lives of others every day whether it be your children, coworkers, friends, or strangers. How you act matters. What you say matters. The way you treat others is important. There might be days when you don't feel like being nice and letting your light shine, but don't let your guard down. Strive to be a positive influence at all times, inside and outside of your home. People around you watch to see how you handle situations. Here are some suggestions on the best ways to have a positive impact on everyone you meet:

- Listen: Paying attention to what others have to say is becoming a lost art. Many times, your mind may drift during a conversation as you think about what you want to say next; consequently, you don't really hear what someone is telling you. Step back and focus directly on what others have to say. They will notice and appreciate that you took the time to concentrate on listening to their ideas and opinions, and you will earn their respect.

- Invest: Take the time to find a way to do something special to give back. When you tweet or message your friends to tell them you will pray for them, do you do it? Take it a step further. Pick up your phone, call them, and pray with them. Put your words into action. Be a mentor and lead by example. Teach someone a skill or make a connection to help a friend find a job. Run an errand for your elderly neighbor. There are many things you can do to invest in the lives of others. "Bear one another's burdens, and so fulfill the law of Christ" (Galatians 6:2).

- Involve: Make room to include your children in your life. Do fun things with them and create memories that will last for a lifetime. Show them character by finding something they can do with you to help others such as yard work for a widow. Invite a coworker to coffee to get to know them. Introduce yourself to a family that has started attending your church. Don't pass by opportunities to be an encouragement to others and make them feel important.

- Lead: You can serve as a guide in many ways. If you are dining with coworkers, bow your head and say a prayer of thanks. Attend church on a regular basis and invite others to come. Lead by example and make this a mandatory expectation for your family. Don't portray church attendance as a burden but as a wonderful opportunity to give thanks to the Creator. Show your children you are excited to go to church and worship God.

- Love: When people see that you genuinely love them and want the best for them, they are more inclined to listen to your advice. But don't offer it unless you are asked, and be ready to back up your answers with Scripture combined with past experience. If you don't know how to help them, point them to a pastor for guidance.

"Beloved, let us love one another, for love is from God, and whoever loves has been born of God and knows God" (1 John 4:7).

Case's father was also a football coach and recruited players who demonstrated solid character. "Those are the men I remember," he said. "Those are the ones who had the most impact on me." At the end of the day, it doesn't matter how much money you make or how many fancy cars you own. Things of the world are nice, but they are not the most important. Your influence and leadership will be what people remember about you.

DAY 2
THERE'S A SCRIPTURE FOR THAT

Teddy Bridgewater
Pro Bowl Quarterback
Carolina Panthers

By Del Duduit

The LORD will keep you from all harm—he will watch over your life; the LORD will watch over your coming and going both now and forevermore.

—Psalm 121:7–8 NIV

Everyone has struggles and challenges in life. Sickness does not discriminate or care if you are a player in the NFL or work a 9-5 job in a small town.

No matter who you are or what you do, chances are you will encounter a problem at some point in your life.

Teddy Bridgewater had some setbacks early in life, but his biggest struggle in life wasn't with something that happened to him. His mother, Rose, fought cancer, and won by the grace of God.

But in those tough days, some of which were grim, he observed how she never lost hope, and it inspired him.

"She told me to never give up hope," he said. "She told me no matter what, to always be happy and stay humble and keep a smile on your face. She always said that."

His mother emphasized Jeremiah 29:11, which gives instruction to have hope for the future.

"That was her main message to me ever since I was a kid growing up," he said. "To always have hope and trust God, because He is the only one who can give you peace."

Teddy also learned the Bible is full of Scriptures that apply to everyday life.

"I had a couple of setbacks early in my life, and I relied on my faith and dove into the Word," he said. "It doesn't matter the circumstance you face, there is a Bible verse to fit that need. There are different ones that apply to different occasions. But it's amazing that you can find one to fit any circumstance."

Teddy's strength and comfort came from within the pages of the Bible, but he was encouraged by the determination of his mother, who fought cancer with grace and toughness.

"You just have to be led by the spirit because the flesh is weak," he added. "You have to depend on the spirit of God for strength and comfort. If your spirit is in line, I think everything else falls into place."

Be still before the LORD and wait patiently for him.
—Psalm 37:7 NIV

In the Huddle

You are not excluded from facing challenging times. Perhaps you have gone through the loss of a job or the end of a special friendship. Maybe you or a loved one have suffered through illness or you are coming off the heels of a tragedy. Where do you find comfort? What verses do you go to in times of trouble? Life is full of ups and downs. But like Teddy said, there are words in the Bible that fit any and every occasion.

Cross the Goal Line

Just because you are a child of the King does not exempt you from heartache. But God promises in His word that He will never leave you or forsake you. You have a choice to let Him comfort you through the blessed Scriptures or try to face the battles alone. Here are some examples of the powerful and healing verses that you can lean on during a trial:

- To overcome fear: Fear is real and can be caused by many circumstances. Perhaps you have lost your job, and you fear the future. Maybe your spouse has passed away, and you fear loneliness. Sickness brings the fear of uncertainty. But you can learn to conquer fear with God's help. "The LORD is my light and my salvation—whom shall I fear? The LORD is the stronghold of my life—of whom shall I be afraid?" (Psalm 27:1 NIV). "For I am the LORD your God who takes hold of your right hand and says to you, do not fear; I will help you" (Isaiah 41:13 NIV).

- To overcome suffering: The Lord has not promised you a life without suffering. You see it every day on the news, or you maybe you are living through it right now. But God did tell you that He will walk with you in the valley. HE will stay by your side and give you grace. "Now if we are children, then we are heirs—heirs of God and co-heirs with Christ, if indeed we share in his sufferings in order that we may also share in his glory. I consider that our present sufferings are not worth comparing with the glory that will be revealed in us" (Romans 8:17–18 NIV).

- To rise above hardships: No one wants to go through battles, but it's part of the journey of life. Teddy's mom did not want to go through cancer, but she faced it with the grace of God. For strength and a guiding light, you can overcome hardships. "Who is it that overcomes the world? Only the one who believes that Jesus is the Son of God" (1 John 5:5 NIV). "Therefore, since we are surrounded by such a great cloud of witnesses, let us throw off everything that hinders and the sin that so easily entangles. And let us run with perseverance the race marked out for us" (Hebrews 12:1 NIV).

- To overcome spiritual attacks: The devil wants you to stumble and take your sights off the Master. But you can fight back with the Word of God: "You intended to harm me, but God intended it for good to accomplish what is now being done, the saving of many lives" (Genesis 50:20 NIV). God will never harm you. "The Lord will rescue me from every evil attack and will bring me safely to his heavenly kingdom. To him be glory for ever and ever. Amen" (2 Timothy 4:18 NIV). The Lord will come to your rescue at the right moment.

Teddy grew to love the Bible and reads it daily. He said God's Word has never changed and has always been his inspiration. He knows where to go when struggles come his way. "I lean on them to help me through the times of turmoil or setback," he said. "Or in life in general. In sad or happy times. All types of things are in there, and there is a Scripture to go along with it. I have to read it every day."

DAY 3
GO TO NINEVEH

Robert Griffin III
Pro Bowl Quarterback
Baltimore Ravens

By Del Duduit

The Lord is not slow to fulfill his promise as some count slowness, but is patient toward you, not wishing that any should perish, but that all should reach repentance.

—2 Peter 3:9

Robert Griffin III, referred to as RG3 by his fans, came into the league with a lot of fanfare and hype.

The Baylor University quarterback was the second pick in the NFL draft in 2012. He was a highly decorated signal caller and won the prestigious Heisman Trophy in 2011 as well as the Associated Press Player of the Year.

But his journey in the NFL has not been what some fans envisioned.

Injuries have played havoc with the talented athlete, and he never lived up to expectations. After four years with the Washington Redskins, he was let go and did not play with any team during the 2015 season.

He signed with Cleveland in 2016 for two seasons but was released in 2017.

"I've faced some tough obstacles over the years," RG3 said. "But through it all, my faith has been solid. I know His grace was there in my life during dark days."

In early 2018, he signed a contract with Baltimore and was named a backup quarterback. Although he was grateful for the opportunity, he was a little discouraged.

"When I came into this league the number two pick, I knew I could do some great things," he said. "So I had to ask myself, 'Why would I want to go somewhere and compete for a number three or four spot?' I knew I could be a starter, but at the same time I felt God telling me to go there."

He likened his attitude with that of Jonah when the Lord told him to go to Nineveh.

Jonah wanted the city destroyed and balked from going. In his heart, he believed that Nineveh deserved God's wrath, and he did not want to see mercy extended to the people.

He soon discovered that the Lord's mercy and salvation is available to all who repent and not to those who Jonah selected.

"I prayed and asked for guidance," RG3 said. "I made the decision to go and earn my spot. Then I got re-signed and continued to work my way back. I know that without God's direction in my life and my faith, I would not be here today. This organization has been good to me."

He has battled back from knee injuries and from going from one team to another, and he knows he can still play at a high level.

"It's just important to be around great coaches and great teammates where you feel welcome," he said. "There is beauty in being accepted by everyone and by God."

> For God gave us a spirit not of fear but of power and love and self-control.
>
> —2 Timothy 1:7

In the Huddle

Have you ever questioned the Lord's leading in your life? Perhaps you want to move to the big city and land the perfect career. You have gone to school and searched for opportunities and have arranged for an interview. Or maybe your heart was set on dating someone who didn't feel the same way. Sometimes we try to write our own story and become discouraged when it doesn't end the way we had hoped. Be assured that God always sees the big picture and knows what's best for you, and he will often rewrite your story to protect you from heartache and trouble.

Cross the Goal Line

You might face disappointment with your story just like RG3 did. He imagined himself a starter but accepted the role of a backup. He knew he could still play. He was reminded of Jonah and how he ran from God's orders to go to Nineveh. Perhaps you have a college degree, but God is calling you to work on the mission field. Maybe you question the leading of the Holy Spirit in your life, and you want to know if what you're feeling is the real deal. How can you know? Here are some suggestions on how to confirm the Master's direction in your life:

- Get out of the way: This will be one of the hardest things to do. After all, you might have prepared years for your life plan but God has a different idea. Don't be a stumbling block to God's design for your future, and don't depend on YOURSELF for the answers. God wants you to depend on HIM. Give in to His will and His way, and don't get ahead of Him. "Commit your way to the LORD; trust in him, and he will act" (Psalm 37:5).

- Seek the Lord's direction: Don't barter with the Lord and tell Him you will do something for Him if He does something for you. It doesn't work that way. Ask what He wants you to do or where He wants to send you. Don't make your plans first and then ask God to bless them. Ask Him to guide and direct you to fulfill His blueprint for your life. "In all your ways acknowledge him, and he will make straight your paths" (Proverbs 3:6).

- Resist temptation and negativity: Avoid people who tell you to follow your gut instincts. Instead, remember that your blessings come from God. Satan tries to make the wrong decisions look glamorous, but turn away and focus on what God wants for you and your family. Concentrate on how your decisions will please the Master, not man. "Be not wise in your own eyes; fear the LORD, and turn away from evil" (Proverbs 3:7).

- Make God your first-round pick: When you put Him first in your life, all things will fall into place. They might not be the overnight results you want, but they will always be what is best. It's okay to listen to friends and family and to ask for advice, but make sure they will pray with you and speak life into you. They should be encouraging you to follow God's will for your future.

- Have peace: Sometimes you may wonder if God cares at all about your situation, especially when life has caused you to fumble your plans. But know in your heart that He does care for you, and He loves you very much. This is why He sent His only Son to die for you. He wants the best for you and will lead you down the right path. Once you have acknowledged this, you can be assured He will provide the peace you need to make it to the goal line. "For the LORD reproves him whom he loves, as a father the son in whom he delights" (Proverbs 3:12).

At first, RG3 questioned God's direction in his heart. But he admitted that following the Lord's leading and going to Baltimore was one of the best decisions he ever made. Follow the Lord's direction, and you will make the game-winning pass.

DAY 4
SURRENDER EVERYTHING TO GOD

Domato Peko
Nose Tackle
Baltimore Ravens, Arizona Cardinals

By Del Duduit

Humble yourselves before the Lord, and he will exalt you.
—James 4:10

Domato Peko is big man. He stands six-feet, three-inches tall and weighs 325 pounds.

You would think a man that big does not need to ask God for strength.

He played most of his career in Cincinnati where he was a mainstay in the defensive starting lineup. He wreaked havoc on the opponents' offensive strategy and made his presence known on the field.

At one time, he was the eight-strongest lineman in the NFL and bench-pressed 225 pounds 25 times at the league's combine.

But he always wanted more. He knew he had to be strong to be successful.

Before each game, fans could always find Domato in the end zone, on his knees with his arms raised to the heavens.

"I had to ask God before every game to give me the strength that He gave to Samson when he defeated the Philistines with the jawbone of an ass," he said. "And I always wanted the courage that He gave to Daniel when he defeated Goliath."

But Domato ended each prayer by asking for God to give him endurance like He gave to His Son, Jesus, when He was hung on the cross.

"I know He provides for me because I can feel it," Domato said. "It's real to me. The power He gives me is real."

He does not pray publicly for show, but instead he wants to be a witness to all who come to see him play.

"I give all the glory to God, and I believe that if I give my best, then I know He will do the rest," he added. "I want everyone to know that I pray to the Lord. As long as I'm out there doing my job, doing my best, He will always give me the extra push to take me over the edge to continue to be successful."

The Michigan State product grew up in church, and his father was a pastor. He learned that family is important and how important it is to be honest and humble.

"I heard the Word of God all the time and love it," he said. "But when I go to the end zone and pray in front of thousands of fans, I am putting my words into action— and actions speak louder. Everyone there sees me lift my arms up and surrender to the Lord."

I appeal to you therefore, brothers, by the mercies of God, to present your bodies as a living sacrifice, holy and accept-able to God, which is your spiritual worship.

—Romans 12:1

In the Huddle

Where do you find your strength to get through each day? Do you allow your problems to consume your thoughts? Does work keep you up at night with worry? Are you afraid to make an appointment with your doctor because you are afraid of what you will find out? Are you scared about things that are out of your control? Do you worry about your children or a relationship? Where do you turn?

Cross the Goal Line

At some point, everyone faces a challenge at work, home, church, school or somewhere else. But do you put God ahead of your obstacles? Do you surrender your problems to the Lord and turn them all over to Him? When you surrender the outcome to God, you give up trying to control your circumstance. This is never an option for an athlete. But to a child of the King, it is essential. It means that you have acknowledged to the Master that you are not big enough to handle your problems, and you need Him to prepare you for battle. When you let go, you give God the room He needs to work. When your arms raise in surrender to the Lord, you become more powerful through His Holy Spirit. Here are some ways to let go and give your situation to God:

- Begin each day on your knees in prayer: Forget about yesterday's penalties and mistakes. Today you have a fresh set of downs to work from. Shake off your worries and rejoice in knowing that God is your quarterback. "Likewise the Spirit helps us in our weakness. For we do not know what to pray for as we ought, but the Spirit himself intercedes for us with groanings too deep for words" (Romans 8:26).

- Begin each day in the Word: Or read during lunch or at the end of the day. The emphasis is to carve out alone time sometime during your day to spend time with God and read His word. Keep a journal and keep track with where you left off the day before. An effective player will know the playbook inside and out. The same goes for the Believer. Read and study God's Word each day. Make this part of your regular routine. "Jesus answered, 'It is written: "Man shall not live on bread alone, but on every word that comes from the mouth of God""" (Matthew 4:4 NIV).

- Surround yourself with encouragement: You cannot make it through this journey alone. One player cannot win the game, and you must rely on your teammates. Choose friends who will inspire you and hold you accountable at the same time. Meet a group of friends for coffee once a month or become involved with a small group who serves God and makes it their goal to share and help each other in this game.

- Find a solid church and stay involved: A team cannot win the game unless it shows up at the stadium. It is very important to your Christian life to attend the house of God and fellowship with others on a regular basis. You expect your favorite player to show up for practice and be in the game. The same goes for you. Go every time you can and not when you want to attend. Don't duck out for a game of golf or to watch a show on TV. Go to church when the doors are open. In these dark times, we need each other more than ever. "Not neglecting to meet together, as is the habit of some, but encouraging one another, and all the more as you see the Day drawing near" (Hebrews 10:25).

Domato faced his challenges head on, but he always asked for strength from the Lord first. He knew he was no match for his opposition without putting God at the front. He knew where his strength came from, and he wanted to make sure his fans were aware that he looked to a higher power. He was a big man but found that he was stronger on his knees.

DAY 5
WHEN THE SHOES DON'T FIT

Demar Dotson
Offensive Tackle
Denver Broncos

By Del Duduit

Commit thy works unto the LORD, and thy thoughts shall be established.

—Proverbs 16:3 KJV

Demar never had any aspirations of playing football. In fact, he had never played the sport in his life.

The six-feet, nine-inch product of Louisiana played basketball at Southern Mississippi all four years. But when his basketball career ended, he still had one year of eligibility left in the NCAA.

He approached the football coach who was reluctant to give him a chance on the gridiron since he had never played in his life.

"He thought it was a little absurd at first," Demar said. "But everyone thought I was a good athlete and a good kid and student with a good reputation. He knew I was a hard worker and decided to give me the opportunity."

Demar played in five games in college, and he enjoyed the newfound sport. When the season ended, he said a simple prayer and asked God to allow one team in the NFL to give him a chance to play at the professional level.

After the draft passed and he was not selected by any teams, he received a phone call from a scout with Tampa Bay.

"Can you come to Tampa right away?" the scout asked.

"No, I can't," Demar replied.

About an hour later, the scout called back and informed him that the team would fly him down for workout with no guarantees of a spot on the roster.

"They wanted to see how it went, and I said yes, I'll come down," he added.

Demar arrived in Tampa but did not think to bring cleats to play on the field. He had imagined an indoor workout and never envisioned a live eleven-on-eleven interaction.

He found the equipment manager and asked if there were any cleats available in size 18.

"The guy kind of yelled at me, then gave me some shoes, but they were size 16," he said. "I wore them during the workout, and they killed my feet and hurt."

The second practice that day, Demar cut out the ends of the shoes for relief.

"Here I was with my toes hanging out," he said. "I kept getting my feet stepped on, and my toes were bleeding."

The next day, Demar laced up his basketball shoes and wore them on the field. He felt better, and his performance improved. In the back of his mind, he remembered his prayer to God: "Just allow one team to give me a chance."

God answered the prayer, and Demar made the squad, against most odds. He only played but one year of college football, and now he had a spot on the roster of an NFL team.

He was considered a solid and productive offensive lineman for the Buccaneers. He stayed at practice late, worked with his coaches, and made the most of his opportunity. He felt that he owed it to the Lord to work hard.

"Without faith and hope you don't have anything," he said. "It's been a great journey for me, but football doesn't define me and who I am."

His belief in Christ on and off the field has got him where he is today. He reached out and trusted the Lord to deliver, and He did.

"I would not trade this journey for anything," he said. "God placed me in Tampa for a reason. I met my wife here in Tampa, and I have beautiful kids, and I have made some wonderful friends. Maybe that's why I'm here."

> And this is the confidence that we have in him, that, if we ask any thing according to his will, he heareth us.
> —1 John 5:14 KJV

In the Huddle

Has God prepared you for something big? Do you trust God enough to put your future in His hands? Sometimes He says "yes" and on occasion, His answer is "no" or "wait." Will you allow Him to prepare you for something big? Perhaps you have a desire to go on a mission trip or maybe you feel the leading of the spirit to quit your job and pursue another direction. The future can be scary because you never know what it holds for you. Demar asked the Lord for a big task—

to allow one team in the NFL to give him a chance. God said "yes," and he made the most of the opportunity. Do you trust the Savior with every detail of your life?

Cross the Goal Line

There is nothing too big for God to handle. This does not necessarily mean you should ask the Lord for six brand new cars to be delivered in your driveway tomorrow (although He could do that). Nor does it mean that you will grow to be the size of Demar and play professional football. If you seek the Lord and His will for and your life, nothing is impossible. But it all comes down to faith and trust and accepting God's will for your life. Here are some ways to trust God for your future:

- You don't have to understand: A friend of mine was in the financial industry most of his professional life. But he knew the Lord was leading him in a different direction, and he was confused because he knew nothing about the area God wanted him to pursue. Finally, he put it in God's hands after much prayer. Today, he is successful in this new venture and uses it as a way to glorify Christ. If Jesus is leading you down a path, you can trust Him to go ahead and follow. "Trust in the LORD with all thine heart; and lean not unto thine own understanding" (Proverbs 3:5 KJV).

- Consider God's character: Think about His love, mercy, and grace in your life. God would never lead you down the wrong path. Don't be afraid. It's okay to question and ask how, but you know you can trust His leading.

- Be aware of His story: Christ died for you and rose again three days later and has prepared a place for you. He will never leave nor forsake you. You can trust Him for your future. "Jesus Christ the same yesterday, and to day, and for ever" (Hebrews 13:8 KJV).

- Be prepared for His answer: God might say yes and take you full steam ahead. He could say no or not now at this time. Or He might say, "Maybe, but let's see what you can do to praise Me first." In all scenarios, you must accept His answer. There might be something you desperately want, but God has something so much better for you. He might even allow you to fail in order to take you the direction that He wants for your life. Be prepared for His answer and give Him all the glory for any success He allows you to have. And when He says "yes," be ready to move into action.

Demar went to the workout unprepared. But when he accepted the challenge, tossed away the shoes that did not fit and used the ones he brought, he thrived and earned a spot on the roster. He had the shoes with him all along that he needed in order to perform well, and once he put them on, he was unstoppable. Go with the tools the Lord sends with you.

DAY 6
TAKE GOD'S WORD WITH YOU

Jarvis Landry
Pro Bowl Wide Receiver
Cleveland Browns

By Del Duduit

> And take the helmet of salvation, and the sword of the Spirit, which is the word of God.
>
> —Ephesians 6:17

When Jarvis Landry goes to work at First Energy Stadium in Cleveland, and when he plays on the road, he brings along the gear he needs to play the game.

He packs his helmet, shoulder pads, cleats, uniform, and everything he will need to perform at the highest level.

But there's another piece of essential equipment he needs for each contest. He also takes along the Word of God everywhere he travels.

"I keep it with me at all times," he said, "especially when I'm on the road. It's a sense of comfort for me knowing that it's in my locker when I'm playing."

Jarvis said he received a Bible as a gift when he was at Louisiana State University, and he treasured it so much that he never leaves it behind.

"Ever since that day, it's been with me. I read it every day," he said. "There is so much negativity in the world, and evil out there, that we have to stay in prayerful mind. That is why I keep it with me all the time. I believe firmly in God."

Jarvis, a five-time Pro Bowl selection, said his mother was his inspiration while he grew up in the South. He knows she would be proud of him today if she were still living, but he takes comfort in knowing he will see her again.

"She is the reason I am a Christian," he said. "She was my hero, and she lived in the church all the time. It was her life. She made us go every Sunday as long as I can remember and talked about her faith. I appreciate that now. She taught me the value of the word of God."

This is one reason why Jarvis takes the Bible with him when he travels. The values inside its pages have been instilled in his heart, and he needs it to guide him through life's journey.

"I wind down and relax when I read the Word of God," he said. "I get courage from reading it."

Jarvis does not keep his faith to himself. He lets everyone who attends a game see his commitment to the Lord.

After the National Anthem is performed, the 2017 NFL reception leader trots down to the two-yard line and gets down on his hands and knees to pray.

"I just put my head on the ground and surrender everything to God," he said. "I don't ask us to win, but I pray for strength and safety and to help me do my best. And I thank Him for everything."

Every word of God proves true; he is a shield to those who take refuge in him.

—Proverbs 30:5

What does the Word of God mean to you?

In the Huddle

What value do you place on the Bible? Does it play a role in every decision you make, or is it just another publication? Does it collect dust in your home? Do you even know where to find it? Do you own one? If so, are you like Jarvis and take it with you whenever you travel? Or do you think it takes up too much room in your suitcase? Have you ever thought about downloading the Bible to your phone or tablet? Do you read the Word of God faithfully each day?

Cross the Goal Line

If you take a vacation to the beach, you bring along the proper attire, beach towels, toys, and other things you will need. If you go on a fishing trip, you pack your poles and gear. When you go on a business trip, you bring your laptop and briefcase with the necessary files you will need for your meetings and presentations. Doesn't it make sense to toss in the source of strength you will need to face each day? Here are some reasons why you need to make sure you have a copy of the Bible with you at all times:

- It is a strong witness: When your neighbors or others see you carry the book, you are sending a message about the importance of God in your life. It might lay the groundwork for a discussion with someone who might observe you with your Bible in an airport. If you have ever sat and waited on a plane, hundreds of people are reading books. Why not let them see you read the inspired Word of God? This might open a window to tell someone about the love of Christ.

- It shows the importance you place on the Bible: There is no greater book than the Bible. It is the most published book in history, and it is read worldwide. The Word was written by a bestselling author, and the stories inside have inspired movies, television shows, and even more books. Don't be ashamed to carry your Bible. Be proud of the heritage it has given you and the light that you shine to those around you. "For the word of God is living and active, sharper than any two-edged sword, piercing to the division of soul and of spirit, of joints and of marrow, and discerning the thoughts and intentions of the heart" (Hebrews 4:12).

- It prepares you for the services you will hear in church: Jarvis Landry must study his playbook with the Browns to be successful. He knows it inside and out. He also reads the Word of God to prepare him for life's battles. Don't depend on your pastor to teach you everything you know. Study ahead of time, and you will appreciate the wisdom you receive in God's house and be in tune with the Holy Spirit more than ever. "Do your best to present yourself to God as one approved, a worker who has no need to be ashamed, rightly handling the word of truth" (2 Timothy 2:15).

- It will help you in a time of trouble: If you ever face a difficult situation and need to find comfort in the

Scriptures, then you will have it on hand. Maybe you can keep one in the glove compartment of your car or in the desk of your office. Problems arise outside the confines of your home so you should consider storing a Bible in multiple locations. Just when you need the Lord and his advice, you will have it within reach. "For whatever was written in former days was written for our instruction, that through endurance and through the encouragement of the Scriptures we might have hope" (Romans 15:4).

Jarvis does not leave for work without his Bible. The Word of God is just as important as the uniform and protective gear he must wear to represent his team. It is the winning playbook and your defense for when Satan and his team try to bring you down. Don't leave home without it.

DAY 7
GO ALONG FOR THE RIDE

Justin Bethel
Pro Bowl Cornerback
New England Patriots

By Del Duduit

I am the good shepherd. The good shepherd lays down his life for the sheep.

—John 10:11

Toward the end of the 2015 season, Justin Bethel injured his ankle in a game against the Cincinnati Bengals.

A few months later, he underwent surgery to repair a broken bone. The decorated special team player's future in the NFL was uncertain.

He had previously earned three trips to the Pro Bowl as a member of the Arizona Cardinals and earned significant playing time as a defensive back.

But when the 2016 season began, he was once again a backup.

He fought his way back, and in November, he earned a starting position against San Francisco and turned in a stellar performance.

But it was during the recovery time from his injury that he relied on his faith to bring him through the doubt and confusion. He considered that all the money, fame, and fans could be gone in the twinkling of an eye.

"I had to think that if this turns out to be an injury that keeps me from playing football, then I have to be okay with that," he said. "I had to realize that if that was what God wanted, then He would still take care of me."

Justin grew up in church in South Carolina, and his father was a minister of music. He played the drums, and was raised in an atmosphere where people loved God. He learned to accept the will of God in his life.

"My outlook and philosophy were always to let the Lord put me in the position I need to be in," he said. "And I just had to put everything in His hands. After I was hurt, I just had to go out there and play and let God take care of me. It's that simple."

Through all the ups and downs, Justin never took his talent and ability for granted.

"Just the fact that I'm in the position I am right now is awesome," he added. "There are a lot of people who want to be where I am now. I'm fortunate enough and blessed enough to be given the talents to go out there and compete and play football at a high level. It's a lot of kids' dreams, and I get to live it every day."

But Justin knows his career could end any day, and he's fine with that.

"I'm along for the ride," he said. "I'll do what I need to do to prepare, and I know that the Lord will take care of me. If I'm playing in the NFL or not, I know He has a plan for me."

Behold, I am with you and will keep you wherever you go, and will bring you back to this land. For I will not leave you until I have done what I have promised you.

—Genesis 28:15

In the Huddle

Have you ever worried that an injury might keep you from playing in the game of life? Maybe you have longed for a job promotion or you have wished for the vacation of a lifetime. But then you are sideswiped by an unexpected layoff or illness and are forced to change course. Surprises may happen at any moment, and your plans could be instantly thrashed by circumstances that are out of your control.

Cross the Goal Line

Justin never planned on breaking his ankle or having surgery to repair it so he could return to his football career in the NFL. He did what he needed to do and put the rest in God's hands. For many, this is easier said than done. But Justin is a good role model to show you the attitude you need to be successful. Do you have the confidence and faith that God can and will take care of you no matter what happens? Here are some practical suggestions to take away your worries and give you peace:

- Stop worrying: Worry and doubt will weigh you down and create a toxic atmosphere that smothers you with negativity. Focus on the positive. Look for inspirational quotes and share them with others on your social media. Search for books to read that are encouraging and uplifting. Concentrate on creating a positive mindset by surrounding yourself with people who are happy, love life, and serve the Lord. "But Jesus looked at them and said, 'With man this is impossible, but with God all things are possible'" (Matthew 19:26).

- Remember the power of God: When you have concerns that you are going to fail, try to recall all the blessings the Lord has already given you in the past. Read about His miracles in the Bible and have faith in the promises of His Word. If He can take care of a sparrow, then He can supply your needs too.

- Pray about your weaknesses: Everyone has vulnerabilities, and Satan will attack you where you are weakest to try to break you. Show common sense by staying away from the people, places, or things that tempt you to sin, and ask the Lord to strengthen you, take away your fears, and give you the power to resist temptation. Acknowledge your weaknesses, and ask God to help you find a way to overcome them. "But he said to me, 'My grace is sufficient for you, for my power is made perfect in weakness.' Therefore, I will boast all the more gladly of my weaknesses, so that the power of Christ may rest upon me" (2 Corinthians 12:9).

- Rejoice: Praising God will help you to be at peace and anticipate the good things God has in store for you. Don't put a timetable on Christ because His plans are always best. Worship Him in the bad times as well as the good. This will assist in healing to strengthen your attitude so you can "go along for the ride" like Justin. "But let all who take refuge in you rejoice; let them ever sing for joy, and spread your protection over them, that those who love your name may exult in you" (Psalm 5:11).

Justin was good with whatever outcome God had in store for him. Maybe the Lord wanted to check his attitude and make sure that he knew who was in charge of his life. Once you set your mind on God and His perfect will for your life, you can get back on the field and return a punt for the game-winning touchdown.

DAY 8
THE LIFE VERSE

Derek Carr
Pro Bowl Quarterback
Las Vegas Raiders

By Del Duduit

For I know the thoughts that I think toward you, says the LORD, thoughts of peace and not of evil, to give you a future and a hope.

—Jeremiah 29:11 NKJV

This verse has a special meaning for Derek Carr, and it is a favorite for many followers of Christ.

The words reflect God's grace for all. He has good plans for all who turn to Him, and these include peace and hope.

Derek's grandfather was a pastor of the same church for more than 30 years. His mother still attends there and leads worship.

"We were all pretty rooted there and some still are," he said. "Our family has gone there for years."

The Fresno State product was close to his grandfather and admired his walk with the Lord. But Derek was confused when his mentor was diagnosed with cancer. He watched him struggle and prayed for his healing.

"Before he passed away, he wanted all of his grandkids to know the verse, Jeremiah 29:11," he said. "We just could not understand at that time why this person—one of the best I'd ever known—was laying there with cancer. It just didn't make any sense to us."

Derek said his grandfather made sure the verse was instilled in his grandchildren, and he wanted them all to know how good God was to him and his family, even in death.

"I loved him for that," Derek said. "Even in the hard times, he wanted us all to know the Lord loved us."

The verse is tattooed on his wrist, and he looks at it every day to remember his grandfather and receive inspiration.

"That verse goes with me everywhere," he said.

Another Scripture Derek clings to is Psalm 91:9–11. "Because you have made the LORD, who is my refuge, even the Most High, your dwelling place, no evil shall befall you, nor shall any plague come near your dwelling; for He shall give His angels charge over you, to keep you in all your ways" (NKJV).

"This is my life verse, because as long as I allow Christ in my life, I know I will be protected," he said. "The most important thing is that I know I have Christ in my heart. Whatever comes my way, I know He will protect my heart."

What is your favorite verse? What meaning does it have in your life?

Rejoice always, pray without ceasing, in everything give thanks; for this is the will of God in Christ Jesus for you.
                    —1 Thessalonians 5:16-18 NKJV

In the Huddle

Have you experienced a major event that makes you reflect and appreciate what you have? Maybe a loved one passed away and left you with a legacy that you will never forget. Perhaps the person who influenced you to follow Christ shared a special verse with you. Maybe during a dark time in your life when you turned to God for answers, He brought you through to victory with a Scripture that helped you to depend on Him. You can often relate to special times in your past with a life verse or two that is important to you.

Cross the Goal Line

Do you have a life verse? Many choose their life verse based on the comfort it brought during sorrow or the joy it gave them in the midst of pain. Our life verses remind us of God's goodness and His saving power. They are the words that have rescued us from heartache and have given us hope for the future. Let your life verse be a compass that draws you back to Him when you experience an emotional or difficult time. Here are some of my favorites I recommend to help give you encouragement along your journey:

- "I can do all things through Christ who strengthens me" (Philippians 4:13 NKJV). This is a popular verse and sums up how many believers feel about their relationship with the Lord. This verse is meant to provide confidence in times of trial or when they face temptation.

- "Let the words of my mouth and the meditation of my heart be acceptable in Your sight, O LORD, my strength and my Redeemer" (Psalm 19:14 NKJV). This verse can serve as a reminder not to say something you will regret. You might fall back on this when you are enticed to get involved in an argument and you don't want to say the wrong thing. It can also be a daily encouragement when you go to work, and you want to be a good example to others.

- "The LORD is my strength and my shield; my heart trusted in Him, and I am helped; therefore, my heart greatly rejoices, and with my song I will praise Him" (Psalm 28:7 NKJV). What better way than to commit to memory Scripture that gives you happiness. And it also brings to the top of your mind who is in charge of your life and who gives you strength.

- "Trust in the LORD with all your heart, and lean not on your own understanding; in all your ways acknowledge Him, and He shall direct your paths" (Proverbs 3:5–6). This verse instructs you to get out of the way and allow the Lord to lead you in your journey. Derek did not understand at the time why his grandfather had cancer, but he had to rely on God for strength to face that trial. You might not understand why you must experience certain events in your life, but trusting God will help you to accept the circumstances and rely on His plan. When trouble comes, use God's word to draw closer to Him.

- "For by grace you have been saved through faith, and that not of yourselves; it is the gift of God, not of works, lest anyone should boast" (Ephesians 2:8–9 NKJV). These words serve as a reminder of to remember to be humble and remember where God has brought you from. You should never boast of your accomplishments, and always give God the glory for your successes in life. When Derek is honored for his work on the field, he always gives credit to his Savior.

There are dozens more excellent examples of life verses that can get you through the tough times. Like Derek, some people need them to stay grounded. God's word is alive and well and can be applied to any situation that may test your faith. Commit your life verses to memory and recite them often. Use them as a valuable resource to strengthen your faith and fight evil.

DAY 9
SPREAD THE MESSAGE

C. J. Uzomah
Tight End
Cincinnati Bengals

By Del Duduit

And he said to them, "Go into all the world and proclaim the gospel to the whole creation."

—Mark 16:15

Millions of people have accounts on Facebook, Instagram, or Twitter. But the majority of them don't have more than a million followers, and their every move is not "liked" or shared to the entire world.

Social media posts are lighthearted and fun, and others are divisive. They can inspire and encourage, or they can go to the other extreme and cause serious damage to people's reputations.

You have a responsibility to those you impact when you have a large platform.

When C. J. Uzomah played at Auburn University, his football coach gave him some good advice.

"He said to use your platform and use your influence in a positive way," C. J. said. "He told me that a lot of young kids looks up to football players to be a positive influence."

The Suwanee, Georgia, native took the recommendation to heart, and he applied it to what he had already learned during his upbringing from his parents and from attending church.

"I was blessed to have two parents who taught me the right way," he said. "There are and always will be struggles, but I have the attitude that it could be a lot worse."

Through all his ups and downs, C. J. likes to spread a message of hope and encouragement through his social media.

"Some guys in the league share a different message than mine," he added. "But I want mine to be a positive message. I am not afraid to admit I'm a Christian and that I believe Jesus Christ is my Savior."

He knows and is aware that he would not be where he is today without the guidance of the Lord, and he never wants to take his blessings for granted.

"I've been given abilities not everyone has and it's for a reason," C. J. said. "I've been put in an amazing situation, and it's our job as believers to harness and use our abilities and our influence in a way that honors Him and lets everyone know about His grace and mercy."

How do you share your witness with your coworkers?

Do your best to present yourself to God as one approved, a worker who has no need to be ashamed, rightly handling the word of truth.

—2 Timothy 2:15

In the Huddle

Maybe you don't have the attention of more than 45,000 people on any given Sunday like C. J. does during the NFL season. But you do have influence on your family, friends, and coworkers. Do they know you love the Lord? Would they be surprised to find out you are a Christian? What is your witness to them? Will they see you go to places you should not be going to after hours? Will they hear words slip from your lips that a follower of God should not say? What can they expect to see on your social media platform?

Cross the Goal Line

You can have a positive impact on those around you and let everyone know you are a Christian without turning people off. It's not hard at all, and in fact, it can be fun. At the same time you are sharing recipes, funny jokes, and pictures of your family, throw in some positive and inspirational messages at the same time. You want to appeal to a wide range of people when you introduce them to the goodness of God. Here are some suggestions for how to be a light in the dark world of social media:

- Treat friends and followers with respect: Many people may not know everyone they interact with on sites such as Twitter. You have an opportunity to earn respect from those who connect with you. Never engage in insensitive dialogue and try to post words of encouragement. Don't hide behind anonymity and say things you wouldn't have the courage to say to someone's face, and always avoid inappropriate relationships.

- Be you: The personality you display on Twitter or Instagram should reflect the real you. As a Christian, you should not be following and liking posts made by those who represent non-virtuous beliefs and ways of life. Absolutely do not use foul language. Be who you are. No one likes someone who is fake, so don't use social media as an alter-ego. "Abstain from every form of evil" (1 Thessalonians 5:22).

- Use your platform to serve others: Don't be concerned with the numbers of people who follow you. Instead, make the followers that you have feel important. When you treat others with respect, kindness, and the love of God, you will attract more friends and followers to your platform.

- Use your unique voice: God made you to be you and didn't intend for you to be an echo chamber. It's okay to share or retweet the thoughts of others whom you admire. But ask God for wisdom to make your own statements of positive influence on those who follow you. Post about how much you enjoyed Sunday School or how much you are looking forward to a revival service, and invite people to attend. If you receive a snarky comment, don't engage. You have done your part to be a witness.

- Let everyone know what you believe: Just a few simple words like, Christian, Believer, Follower of Christ, will get the message out clear. "For I am not ashamed of the gospel, for it is the power of God for salvation to everyone who believes, to the Jew first and also to the Greek" (Romans 1:16).

- Let your light shine: Capitalize on opportunities to tell others about the Savior. Keep your posts positive with a mix of spiritual inspiration and uplifting items about your day. Nobody wants to read about your problems, and long detailed rants will lose readers in a heartbeat. It's fine to share happy news about your family, a picture of your favorite meal, and even clean humor. Prayer requests are fine too, but take the time to share about the saving grace of God and how happy you are to be a Christian. Mix it up. "When they see your respectful and pure conduct" (1 Peter 3:2).

C. J. was inspired by his college coach to be a positive influence on his team and fans. God expects you to do the same. Social media is a valuable tool to help you take a public stand for Jesus.

DAY 10
IT'S NOT ABOUT YOU

Justin Simmons
All-Pro Free Safety
Denver Broncos

By Del Duduit

> Let each of you look not only to his own interests, but also to the interests of others.
>
> —Philippians 2:4

Players in the National Football League are perceived to live a lavish lifestyle.

According to completepayroll.com, the average salary in 2018 for a professional football player was $2.7 million, while the average American makes around $63,000 per year.

Fans see their favorite players drive fancy cars and live in huge mansions. They also see reports about players who mismanage their income and are broke soon after retirement.

Some All-Star players receive the royal treatment, and admirers flock to them for pictures and autographs.

The stigma is something Justin Simmons sees, but he does not appreciate. He is thankful for his job, but he is not a fan of the limelight.

"The NFL is so focused on you, you, you and what you can do and what you can produce," he said. "You get paid a lot of money and get endorsements which is more money and it's all about you, you, you."

But as a Christian, Simmons knows his life is not about him. It's about Him.

"We all have a common goal and that is to win. That's what we are paid to do," he said. "We had to be selfish to some point on the field, but it's just the opposite when it comes to faith. We are taught as Christians not to be selfish, right?"

Simmons, who played football at Boston College and was second team All-Pro for Denver in 2019, said he struggles with the separation of faith and being selfish on the field.

"That's my biggest struggle really," he said. "Faith to me is about serving others and loving on others and helping them out."

He said as a whole, some professional athletes don't live up to those standards.

"We are in a system, in a locker room with a bunch of guys—not necessarily on this team—in general where it's a bunch of selfish players and it's all about me, me, me. It's about the largest contract or it's about getting the headline. Internally, you tend to fall into that trap and make it all about you, and it's hard to stay disciplined, but I have to stay grounded in my faith."

Simmons, who grew up in Virginia, said he was blessed to play for Denver because the Broncos uphold the "team" concept where selfishness is discouraged.

He said he relies on the team chaplain and other Christians on the team, as well as his wife, to keep him focused.

"It's all about helping each other and making sure we all look out for each other," he added. "My community and my church are what I lean on besides my family and teammates. My faith is important to me, and I never want to put myself up on a pedestal because sooner or later, you'll come crashing down."

Do you seek attention from others and seek the limelight?

Where do you place "you" on your roster?

He must increase, but I must decrease.

—John 3:30

In the Huddle

In today's society, you do your best to stay ahead and provide for your family. There is nothing wrong with hard work and being honored or recognized for your accomplishments. But perhaps you are obsessed with winning the "Employee of the Year Award" or landing the corner office with the view. Perhaps you do more than is expected and crave the applause from your colleagues or supervisors. When it becomes all about you instead of the team, then you must examine your priorities.

Cross the Goal Line

Maybe you have been so distracted by your career or hobbies that you have misplaced priorities. Perhaps you are so focused on your own success that you have no concern for the plight of others. God instructed us to have a charitable heart. Here are some ways to consider putting the needs of others in front of yours and why that's important:

- Give your tithes: God commands that you give back at least ten percent of what you earn. Some are convicted to base this on their gross pay before the government takes its share. Give your offering to God on a regular basis. The Lord will bless and honor your dedication. Churches use tithe money to help their local communities, support missionary work, and serve others, and your giving allows you to be a part of these efforts. "Honor the LORD with your wealth and with the first-fruits of all your produce" (Proverbs 3:9).

- Volunteer in your community: There are countless non-profit organizations looking for people to donate their time. A few examples are the Red Cross, the United Way, or Big Brothers/Big Sisters. You can become involved in youth activities or sports and become a mentor in your area. You can help out as a volunteer at a local hospital or food bank and help others in need. "In all things I have shown you that by working hard in this way we must help the weak and remember the words of the Lord Jesus, how he himself said, 'It is more blessed to give than to receive'" (Acts 20:35).

- Go on a mission trip: This is a wonderful way to put your concern for the needs of others into action. Do some research to find those organizations that travel to other countries, or find projects even within your own community or state that attend to the needs of others, such as Habitat for Humanity. You don't have to travel across the world to make an impact. Maybe your mission trip is to be of service to a widow down the street who needs her lawn mowed. Sometimes the ones who need the most help will never ask, so ask God to guide you to someone who needs assistance or ask your church leaders for suggestions. "But if anyone has the world's goods and sees his brother in need, yet closes his heart against him, how does God's love abide in him?" (1 John 3:17).

Justin has the right perspective. He must perform his job at the highest level if he wants to keep playing. He likes to win, but he realizes there are eleven players on the field. To him, he plays as a member of the team and does not care if his name appears in bright lights or not. The only letter he is concerned with is the W for winner. When you put the needs of others above your own, then you can sleep at night with a clear conscience, knowing that your priorities are in order and you helped to make a difference.

DAY 11
IT'S YOUR CHOICE

Robert Griffin III
Pro Bowl Quarterback
Baltimore Ravens

By Del Duduit

"Then spake Jesus again unto them, saying, I am the light of the world: he that followeth me shall not walk in darkness, but shall have the light of life."

—John 8:12 KJV

Robert Griffin III was raised in church, and his family finally settled in Copperas Cove, Texas, after both of his parents retired from service to our country. Known as RG3, he learned right from wrong as a child.

"My mom and dad guided me and taught me in the way of the church," he said. "But there comes a time in your life when you have to make the decision on your own, you know if you want to follow the Lord."

At the age of 13, RG3 chose God. Life was good, and he had a bright future ahead of him. In high school, he was a standout athlete in football and track and was highly recruited by major colleges.

He settled on Baylor University and went on to achieve many awards during his college career. He was the Big 12

Offensive Freshman of the Year in 2008 and piled up the honors. In 2011, he won the Manning Award, the *Sporting News* Player of the Year, the Davey O'Brian Award, and the prestigious Heisman Trophy.

But during his freshman year, he struggled for a few weeks with his salvation.

"I felt like I was doing everything right. I was living the right way and living the life God asked me to live," he said. "But I was experiencing hardships for the first time and didn't know how to deal with it."

For about two weeks, he was confused.

"I just questioned everything," he said. "My faith was weak, and I had doubts about my life."

He remembers seeking the Lord in prayer for guidance.

"It was the first time I had to make the decision to follow God as a man," he said. "And not because someone told me to or that it was the cool thing to do. I made the decision because I truly believe in Him and have faith in Him. I came out of my trial more convicted and stronger in my faith than ever."

After he entered the NFL, he experienced more discouragement from injuries as well as getting traded and cut from teams.

But then he found a home in Baltimore and accepted his role as a non-starter. Although he went through personal and professional struggles, he maintained his faith.

"If we go out and play a great game and I have a bad play, it bothers me," he said. "But I know it's not because I'm not living right or following God's plan. It's because it's a learning experience, and when adversity comes into your life, you have to be able to qualify it and still have the faith that God's plan for you will move you ahead."

> And the Lord direct your hearts into the love of God, and into the patient waiting for Christ.
> —2 Thessalonians 3:5 KJV

Are you moving forward? What decisions have you made, and have you included God in your plans?

In the Huddle

Perhaps you can identify with RG3. Maybe you were raised in church where you learned right from wrong. Maybe you went to college and was overwhelmed with the changes in your life. Did you have the courage to seek the Lord and ask for direction? What choices did you make? Did you seek the Lord and follow His ways, or did you stumble because you tried to take care of it on your own?

Cross the Goal Line

No matter the circumstances, it is never too late to ask Christ to save you from your sins and to lead you in the right paths. You might be in college or facing challenges at work and are unsure about which way to turn. Perhaps you have regrets about the way you have treated others. Rest assured time has not expired. You can still make the right play and seek a touch from the Master. Here are some things to consider when you make important choices:

- God is always sovereign: Focus on asking God for discernment each day regarding what lies ahead. You are faced with choices every day, and you may sometimes make the wrong one. When you make mistakes, take them to the Lord in prayer and ask for His forgiveness and guidance. Never try to hide from your decisions, but rather take responsibility. "He that covereth his sins shall not prosper: but whoso confesseth and forsaketh them shall have mercy" (Proverbs 28:13 KJV).

- Trust God that your situation will work out for the best: The Lord can turn a bleak situation into a positive outcome that you could never have imagined. This doesn't mean God's children are problem-free. But it means you have hope in the Lord that He will always take you down the right path. You may have lost your job, but you put in for another one that turns out to be better for you and your family. Or perhaps a relationship ends because God now has the perfect person ready that He has prepared for you. Everything that happens to you is for your good. "And we know that all things work together for good to them that love God, to them who are the called according to his purpose" (Romans 8:28 KJV).

- Make His plans your plans: Once you commit to letting the Lord have His way in your life, things will begin to work out. Your idea of success might be different than Gods. But He sees the big picture, and His plan is always better than yours. So, it's best not to concern yourself with the details. Focus on placing your full trust and hope in His will.

- Find people you trust and ask for their advice: When you are faced with a tough decision, seek wise counsel from people who have been in your situation. Invite your pastor for a cup of coffee or spend time with a group of friends who share similar dreams. A different perspective is always good and could be the key to unlocking the answers. "Hear counsel, and receive instruction, that thou mayest be wise in thy latter end" (Proverbs 19:20 KJV).

- Expect the impossible: When you need God the most, He comes through when you least expect it to happen. Have faith and take your needs to Him in prayer. When you are at your weakest point and on your knees, He sees and honors your humility.

Robert said he struggled for a short time in college before he realized that God was bigger than his fears. He came out on the other side stronger and more confident in his relationship with the Lord. His life has not been perfect, and he has made poor decisions, but he always knows to go to God to make things right.

DAY 12
DO YOUR BEST TO SUPPORT OTHERS

C. J. Uzomah
Tight End
Cincinnati Bengals

By Del Duduit

Give, and it will be given to you. Good measure, pressed down, shaken together, running over, will be put into your lap. For with the measure you use it will be measured back to you.

—Luke 6:38

Everyone has struggles in life. There are many ups and downs. Some discouraging events might not seem big to others, yet they are significant to you.

Obstacles can range from health issues, to financial problems, or finding employment. These hurdles can happen at any time, and they seem to come when you are not prepared.

Football fans in the Queen City don't think of problems when they watch C. J. Uzomah play ball.

They see a tight end who is well compensated for his talent and ability.

But even the six-feet six-inch 265-pound receiver has his own unique problems. He doesn't dwell on them because they can bring down his spirits.

"I'm blessed to be in the position I am right now with the Bengals and in the league," he said. "We all have struggles, and it's insane for me to think about them all the time. I think the hardest part for me honestly is not comparing my life and my walk with others. This is my journey."

He is aware that he was blessed with Christian parents who instilled within him a humble attitude and encouraged him to live right in the sight of God.

This inspired him to face his battles head on knowing the Lord was on his side.

"Every day we face struggles, but I don't look at them as struggles," he said. "I take the approach that things could be worse. I'm alive and I am blessed to be where I am. I don't take it for granted because I have worked hard."

He noted the best way he deals with issues is to turn it over to the Lord and rely on his circle of family and friends for support.

"I have a wonderful support system in place with people who love me," he said. "That means everything. To be able to confide in people who believe the same way you do is helpful."

One person C.J. looks to when he is down is his girlfriend. She sends him a Bible verse every day to encourage and inspire him.

"I love that," he said. "Just to know people think of you enough to pray for you is amazing. And I have a great support system on my team too—and that makes it easier."

Are you there for your friends? Do you support them?

> We who are strong have an obligation to bear with the failings of the weak, and not to please ourselves.
>
> —Romans 15:1

In the Huddle

Are you there when a friend needs you? Do you take time if someone you know is struggling and asks for your support? How do you respond? When colleagues ask you to pray for them, do you? Or do you just go through the motions and brush it off? People have real problems that might not seem big to you, but they are huge to those experiencing the trial. Are you the type of person who will send out an encouraging note or text, or do you keep to your own business?

Cross the Goal Line

Maybe a friend is having a personal struggle at work and wants to meet with you over coffee to vent to you about a problem. Sometimes, it is wise to not get involved or take sides, but rather share with them how you have dealt with similar problems in the past. There is no harm in listening, but be cautious about offering a solution. Instead, pray with them to ask God to provide hope in their situation. Do your best to be open and available for help, but don't let others take advantage of your generosity. Here are some ways you can be there for your loved ones and friends who might be in a struggle:

- Establish boundaries from the start: You must do what
  you can to build strong friendships with both Christians and non-believers. But at the same time, you must
  be wise. When you set boundaries, not only to protect
  you and the others involved. Never counsel a member
  of the opposite sex in person without witness, and don't
  let it interfere with your personal or family time. Let
  them know you can offer ideas, encouragement, and
  suggestions for a solution, but the ultimate decision is
  up to them. "Let your foot be seldom in your neighbor's house, lest he have his fill of you and hate you"
  (Proverbs 25:17).

- Show honor and respect: Never downplay someone's
  problems, even if you might think they are petty. View
  others in high regard and treat them how you want
  to be treated. Make sure you value their situation and
  let them know how much you care. "Whoever belittles
  his neighbor lacks sense, but a man of understanding
  remains silent" (Proverbs 11:12).

- Never judge: The last thing you want to do is cast judg-
  ment on the person or their situation. Who knows? You
  might find yourself facing a similar scenario someday if
  you are not careful. Appreciate the time you have and
  acknowledge the courage the person has taken to con-
  sult with you. Uplift and never tear down. "Be kind to
  one another, tenderhearted, forgiving one another, as
  God in Christ forgave you" (Ephesians 4:32).

- Support: A true friend will tell the good and the bad.
  Don't be a rubber stamp and approve something that
  you know is wrong. Instead, remind them to seek forgiveness from God and others. Support their wishes to
  change their ways and give them encouragement for

difficult challenges. Let them know that God will for-give, but it's their responsibility to make changes. "A friend loves at all times, and a brother is born for adver-sity" (Proverbs 17:17).

Being a good friend takes a lot of patience and character. It's also a great opportunity to be a light in a dark situation. Inspire your friends and colleagues to look to Christ as the only way to remedy their problems. Serving God does not mean you will live a problem-free life, you're Christian friends are the best ones to turn to in times of crisis.

DAY 13
BORN TO LOSE, BUILT TO WIN

Tyrod Taylor
Super Bowl Champion Quarterback
Los Angeles Chargers

By Del Duduit

Let all bitterness, wrath, anger, clamor, and evil speaking be put away from you, will all malice.

—Ephesians 4:31 NKJV

Tyrod Taylor has experienced both frustration and jubilation in the NFL.

His happy time came when he was part of the Baltimore team that won a Super Bowl at the end of the 2012 season.

From there he went to play in Buffalo where he enjoyed success as a starter. He was selected to the Pro Bowl in 2017, but he declined the invitation due to an injury.

During the next season, he was benched, and he did not understand why.

"I took the blame for some things that were not entirely my fault," he said. "I don't point fingers for something I did not agree with, and a lot of people didn't agree with. But that is how it goes sometimes, and you just deal with it."

He spent the next year in Cleveland and then hopped to the Chargers in Los Angeles.

Life can be tough in the NFL, but Tyrod has leaned on his faith and avoided bitterness. "Without my faith I think I would have folded," he said. "Some situations are harder than others. I think God puts you through moments or allows things to happen to put you to the test. I think He wants to see how you rely on Him in situations."

Circumstances in life may cause you to throw an interception at a critical moment. But the Lord is always there to make the stop before the opponent goes in for the score.

"I have a great foundation and support system," Tyrod said. "My faith in God gives me a great chance to succeed in life."

Tyrod has a tattoo on his arm that reads: "Born to Lose, Built to Win."

"You have to deal with disappointments and move on with God's grace," he said. "You can't get bitter."

> For I see that you are poisoned by bitterness and bound by iniquity.
>
> —Acts 8:23 NKJV

There is no place in your life to harbor resentment, and it will only cause you to lose your victory. Are you bitter about things that have happened to you in your past?

In the Huddle

Bitterness begins as emotional or spiritual pain that you allow to fester and grow inside of you. The anger turns into animosity. If left unchecked, it could develop into anxiety, depression, or feelings of hostility and hatred. It could poison your life with a desire to get revenge, affecting your health and sleep and harming your relationships. But mostly, it will rob you of happiness and joy and invite you to accept the role of a victim. Your mind will be consumed with harmful thoughts and take away your peace. Has someone hurt you to the point you harbor these feelings? Maybe a former friend told a lie about you, or a co-worker set you up and caused you to lose your job. There are many scenarios that could come into play. But you cannot allow bitterness to take over your life.

Cross the Goal Line

Being happy and content is your choice. It can only be found with the love of Christ in your life. Without it, bitterness and hatred will know no boundaries. But you are better than this. You cannot allow the resentment to creep into your mind and take over your life. If the following are true for you, seek to make some positive changes in your life:

- You talk negatively about certain people: This can be a self-defense move that makes you temporarily feel better for a short time. You spout off or complain to your friends about the person who hurt you. When you are not able to get back at someone, you attack them with words.

- You relive painful memories in your mind all the time: Perhaps you can't forget the hurtful words someone said to you, or someone was dishonest and stabbed you in the back. When you let these events consume your thoughts, you must ask God for the power to forgive.

"Brethren, I do not count myself to have apprehended; but one thing I do, forgetting those things which are behind and reaching forward to those things which are ahead" (Philippians 3:13 NKJV). You cannot change the past. But you can control how it impacts your future.

- You rejoice when others fail: Never take delight when a person who hurt you falls. If you celebrate their misfortune, you need a change in heart. You should never take delight when something bad happens to someone who has wronged you.

- You experience anger when a person's name is mentioned: Do you grit your teeth or become frustrated at the mere mention of a person's name? You don't have to spend time with them, but if just hearing about them upsets you, check yourself and ask God to give you self-control over your reactions.

- You complain and play the victim all the time: You don't have to be thankful for the negative moments in life, but you do need to ask God to lift you out of the despair and help you to stop feeling sorry for yourself. Be grateful for the life God has given you and His promises to take care of you. Stop complaining about your life situation and turn your situation over to the Lord. "In everything give thanks; for this is the will of God in Christ Jesus for you" (1 Thessalonians 5:18 NKJV).

There is healing from bitterness. Ask God to make your heart tender and help you to show kindness to others. Forgive those who hurt you, even if they have never asked you to, as this will release you no matter if they choose to make things right or now. Accept the circumstances and move on with your life. Pray for the person who has offended you, and maybe they will see the light of Christ in your life. You can also seek Christian or professional counselors to help you deal with negative emotions. Chances are, someone will hurt you at some point. But it's up to you to fall back on the grace of God and gain the first down to move on. "Create in me a clean heart, O God, and renew a steadfast spirit within me" (Psalm 51:10 NKJV).

DAY 14
BE THANKFUL

Mark Ingram Jr.
Pro Bowl Running Back
Houston Texans

By Del Duduit

> Giving thanks always and for everything to God the Father
> in the name of our Lord Jesus Christ.
>
> —Ephesians 5:20

The wonderful thing about being a follower of Christ is that He forgives. The Lord is faithful in good times and in difficult situations.

On May 8, 2018, Mark Ingram Jr. knew he had a suspension coming from the NFL for violating league policies on using performance enhancing drugs.

He prepared himself and asked the Lord to forgive him and provide another chance for him to make it right.

"God is good all the time," he said. "And I'm fortunate enough, because I grew up in a home where my mother, father, and grandparents had me in church at a young age. It was tough knowing I had a suspension coming, but my faith was constant, and I tried to see what the Lord had in store for me and what He was trying to tell me."

A fundamental upbringing and exceptional talent guided him to Alabama, where he was an outstanding player.

He captured several awards, which included the *Sporting News* Player of the Year and the Heisman Trophy in 2009. He also guided the Crimson Tide to a BCS National Championship that same year.

The New Orleans Saints took Mark in the first round, and he played in the Big Easy from 2011–2018.

He sat out the first four games of his final season in New Orleans due to the suspension.

"No Christian is perfect, and we all can work to strive to be better and be more like Him every day," he said. "I am so thankful that the Lord has given me this opportunity to play football. He's given me a great family that supports me, a great team. I love my journey with Christ one day at a time."

When his tenure in New Orleans ended, he found himself in Baltimore.

In week 10 against Cincinnati in 2018, Mark was in the backfield alongside Lamar Jackson and Robert Griffin III, marking the first time in the history of the NFL where three former Heisman Trophy winners lined up together for one play.

Through his NFL career, Mark knows he needs to stay thankful in order to be successful. He is grateful for forgiveness and salvation available only through Christ Jesus.

"The Lord forgives, and all you have to do is believe in Him and ask Him to save you," he said. "Believe in Him, walk with Him, and let Him carry your cross every day. I'm so thankful for His blessings on me and my family."

Mark grew up in church and was taught to revere God. His journey in football has been decorated, and he is grateful for his accomplishments.

But he is also thankful that God forgives and extends His mercy.

What are you thankful for in life?

> Praise the LORD! Oh give thanks to the LORD, for he is good, for his steadfast love endures forever!
>
> —Psalm 106:1

In the Huddle

Ask yourself this simple question: Are you thankful? Or is your life so hectic that you lose sight of your blessings and take them for granted? When was the last time you gave God thanks for good things he has given you such as your family, church, good health, and a job? What happens if you hit hard times and struggle financially without a job? Or maybe you are facing a health crisis? Are you still thankful?

Cross the Goal Line

Life can be as fun as winning the Super Bowl or it can be as frustrating as fumbling the football to lose a game. But no matter what challenges you face, you should always be thankful for your blessings. While you might not realize it at the time, God often allows trials to prepare you for something bigger and better. Here are some ways to show Him how thankful you truly are:

- Through a journal: One way to recognize your blessings is to write them down every day. Make a list of three new things each day that God has done for you. Go back at the end of each week and reflect. You will be amazed at how He has touched your life.

- Through your devotions: Once a week, use your private devotion time to just thank the Lord for all He has done. No requests. No favors. No deals. Just give Him praise. "Likewise the Spirit helps us in our weakness. For we do not know what to pray for as we ought, but the Spirit himself intercedes for us with groanings too deep for words" (Romans 8:26).

- Through worship services: Stand to your feet and lift your arms in service and let Him know you thankful you are. You don't need words because actions speak louder. "Let them praise your great and awesome name! Holy is he!" (Psalm 99:3).

- Through appreciation during tough times: Be grateful for your blessings even in difficult situations. When you enter a trial, thank the Lord for His strength and His promises.

- Through witnessing: Make sure you tell your co-workers and friends how good God has been and will be to you and your family. You can slip it in during a normal conversation or you can post it on social media. "Do your best to present yourself to God as one approved, a worker who has no need to be ashamed, rightly handling the word of truth" (2 Timothy 2:15).

When Mark went through a personal and professional struggle, he relied on his faith and was grateful for God's mercy and love. He did not take the second chance for granted and makes sure to praise the Lord every day. Be thankful for everything you have. God has blessed you, and He deserves to be thanked.

DAY 15
VALUE YOUR MARRIAGE

Rigoberto Sanchez
Punter
Indianapolis Colts

By Del Duduit

House and wealth are inherited from fathers, but a prudent wife is from the LORD.

—Proverbs 19:14

Rigoberto Sanchez and Cynthia met at a community college in California. Both were athletes. He played football, and she played soccer.

They had an instant attraction.

She was spunky and he was humble.

Rigoberto had a dream to play in the National Football League, but he needed to play on a bigger stage to catch the eyes of scouts.

He decided to transfer to Hawaii, and she went along for the ride.

"I worked my butt off to practice, and she was right there the whole time, helping me, shagging balls, encouraging me," he said. "Her support for me was tremendous."

No teams showed any real interest in his ability, and it wore on his emotions.

"She kept telling me it was going to happen," he said. "She was my rock the whole time."

In 2017, his dream came true when the Indianapolis Colts signed him as an undrafted free agent.

Cynthia was the first person to find out before the news spread. They realized the magnitude of the journey. He went from obscurity to a roster spot on a team with the NFL.

His rookie season was productive. He beat out a veteran punter for the starting spot and set an NFL record for punting by a rookie with a 42.6-yard-per-punt average.

The Pro Football Writers Association selected him to the All-Rookie Team the same year.

In 2019, the Colts signed him to a lucrative four-year deal, which validated his hard work. But he acknowledges the role his partner in life played in making this happen.

"She has been my biggest influence," he said of Cynthia. "She was there for me when it was dark, and I was in a tunnel."

The couple married soon after his rookie season and together, they make a dynamic duo. "God has blessed us so much," Rigoberto added. "My family brought me up right, and we follow the Lord. And he brought the right lady in my life to encourage me. I get to live my dream with the woman I love who supports me in everything I do."

Rigoberto refers to Cynthia as his backbone and credits her with keeping him focused.

"She's always been behind the scenes and gave me emotional and spiritual support," he said. "She loves to do the little things that help me. She's awesome."

He who finds a wife finds a good thing and obtains favor
from the LORD.

—Proverbs 18:22

Do you value your marriage? How do you treat your partner?

In the Huddle

Maybe you have been married for 25 years or longer or
perhaps you are just starting your journey as a newlywed.
Perhaps you are still searching for the special person God
has prepared for you, or you getting ready to pop the question to the love of your life. In all cases, how do you view
the special person in your life? Do you support them in
their dreams, or do you put your needs and ambitions first?
Would you drop everything to help your partner reach his
or her goals, or do you selfishly pursue your own motives?

Cross the Goal Line

Marriage is fun, but it also takes a lot of work and dedication. There will be times of joy and happiness along with
discouragement and disappointment. During the journey,
it might be easy to lose focus on your commitment. Life has
a way of trying to block a punt and run it back for a score.
But there are ways to strengthen your front line to ensure
this does not happen. Here are some techniques to review
in the film room and strengthen your bond with the person
God has given or will give to you:

- Show respect: This is always in order, but even more so when your children are watching. Little ears and eyes hear and see what goes on in the home. Men and women of faith should demonstrate honor and respect to their spouses. Never berate them or make them feel less of a person. Pray with them, attend church together, and work as a team.

- Show love: Do your best to nurture and cherish your mate. There might be circumstances out of your control, but always show your affection and dedication. Understand their needs and be their biggest support system. "Husbands love your wives, as Christ loved the church and gave himself up for her" (Ephesians 5:25).

- Show flexibility: If your spouse needs you to help with a project, and you made plans to be with friends, then make the right choice and help your partner. Be willing to toss your ego aside and assist in the needs of your best friend. It's all about give and take.

- Show attention: Small acts that seem insignificant to you might be big to your partner. A simple call or two throughout the day or a surprise gift delivered to the office will let them know how much you care. Help each other around the house and share responsibilities.

- Show devotion: This is true in all situations—through the good and bad. There might be emotional, physical, or financial issues to deal with in life. Honor your spouse and let them know you are ready to do whatever it takes to make them happy. Remain faithful and true to each other, and God will bless your relationship. "An excellent wife who can find? She is far more precious than jewels" (Proverbs 31:10).

Cynthia dropped everything to go with Rigoberto to support him in his mission to play in the NFL. She helped him, encouraged, and prayed for him. The Lord honored their hard work and dedication. Teamwork is essential to win the game of life. You might be in the first quarter of your experience, and you have a long way to go and a lot of game left to play. Don't be afraid to punt once in a while and give your team good field position.

DAY 16
FIND YOUR PASSION

Mike Tomlin
Head Coach, Super Bowl Champion
Pittsburgh Steelers

By Del Duduit

> Therefore, my beloved brethren, be ye stedfast, unmoveable, always abounding in the work of the Lord, forasmuch as ye know that your labour is not in vain in the Lord.
> —1 Corinthians 15:58 KJV

Anyone who knows anything about the National Football League is aware that Pittsburgh Steelers Head Coach Mike Tomlin is passionate.

He is a no-nonsense leader who gets to the point quickly and does not like to hypothesize.

I witnessed this one Sunday afternoon in Cincinnati when a reporter posed a scenario to him that was totally unrelated to his team's dramatic last-second win over the Bengals.

"Does anyone have a question that has to do with what just happened on the field?" he said.

He is also a man of conviction and when asked, he makes it clear where he stands on issues. He loves his job and is a man of deep-rooted faith.

At age 36, he became the youngest coach in NFL history to win a Super Bowl when he guided the Steelers to a 27-23 win over Arizona in 2009.

But he has a deeper passion.

A few years ago, he and his wife, Kiya, saw a documentary about teenagers who were abducted and trafficked in the sex slave industry.

This made his blood boil because the couple has three children of their own.

He put his money where his convictions are and became involved in Operation Underground Railroad, which fights against this evil and disgusting empire.

The organization is comprised of former law enforcement officers, special agents, and Navy SEALs and assists local law enforcement perform stings to rescue children from the dark side.

"It's shocking how significant this fight is," he said. "There is no more important fight going on the world right now than this. Our kids."

Mike feels the Lord has put it on his heart to do something besides sit back and watch the news.

"I have a daughter," he said. "It's a fight worth fighting. There are a lot of causes out there that can divide us, but this is not one of them. I cannot find a man who would stand against this. Not one."

This is his calling and passion, he added.

"There are many different causes out there and things that are important to others, and I get that," Mike said. "But any man who cannot get behind this … I don't know about them."

For God is not unrighteous to forget your work and labour of love, which ye have shewed toward his name, in that ye have ministered to the saints, and do minister.
—Hebrews 6:10 KJV

In the Huddle

What are you passionate about? Do you put your actions where your mouth is? Have you ever wanted to do more but did not know what to do, or who to help? Do you have a servant's heart? There are many outstanding organizations that need volunteers to help support worthy causes. Some support mission fields in other countries, and others are right in your back yard.

Cross the Goal Line

You have sat on the sidelines too long. It's time to get into the game and make a difference. The time to act is now. There are many ways to become involved with charitable foundations.

Consider how much time or resources you can give. But first pray and ask God for guidance and direction for a door to open. Here are some causes to consider if you want to do more than sit back and watch from the sidelines:

- Pro-life chapters: Many states have organized these through various cities and counties. Many of them are understaffed, overworked, and looking for volunteers. This cause is not for the faint of heart; even if you do not volunteer, you can sign up to receive communications from your local chapter so you will continue to be completely informed in other ways you can help. "Before I formed thee in the belly I knew thee; and before thou camest forth out of the womb I sanctified thee, and I ordained thee a prophet unto the nations" (Jeremiah 1:5 KJV).

- Mission trips: Many reputable groups organize trips abroad to help share the gospel to people in other countries who have never heard of the love of Christ. Sometimes these are medical missions, or if you like to work with your hands, you can help to build wells or construct a church. This is a labor of love.

- Food banks: You can make an impact in your own community by donating time to local homeless shelters or soup kitchens. You can also organize food drives to help keep them stocked or drop off a monetary donation. "If I then, your Lord and Master, have washed your feet; ye also ought to wash one another's feet" (John 13:14 KJV).

- Disaster relief: Organizations like the American Red Cross or Samaritan's Purse help those who have been impacted by fires, floods, tornados, earthquakes, or even pandemics. This is a wonderful way to help and spread the love of God at the same time. If you can't volunteer your time to assist these organizations, then support them with donations to help them with the supplies they need to provide relief to those who are impacted.

- Children's hospitals: Volunteering at a hospital that supports treatment of children can be a blessing. You may also consider helping out at a Ronald McDonald's home or similar establishment that provides affordable lodging to family members whose children are being treated for long-term illnesses. This type of work can tug on your heart strings, but God can help you brighten the situation for those who are going through difficult trials.

I have shewed you all things, how that so labouring ye ought to support the weak, and to remember the words of the Lord Jesus, how he said, It is more blessed to give than to receive.

—Acts 20:35 KJV

And the list goes on. The point is to find a cause that creates passion within you and stirs you to make a difference. Don't be a one-time wonder. Find a cause, get involved, and stay committed.

DAY 17

SHINE THE BEST YOU CAN FOR GOD

Tim Tebow
Quarterback, Retired
New York Jets

By Del Duduit

> In all things I have shown you that by working hard in this
> way we must help the weak and remember the words of the
> Lord Jesus, how he himself said, "It is more blessed to give
> than to receive."
>
> —Acts 20:35

When Tim Tebow heard about a "Jesus Prom," he thought
it was a fantastic idea.

The Tim Tebow Foundation was about to turn five years
old, and Tim wanted to do something special to mark the
occasion. He wanted to go all out and let everyone know
what it was all about.

The executive director for his foundation knew about
the "Jesus Prom" that was held each year for people with
special needs to have their own night dedicated to just
them.

Tim has a unique desire to help and serve people who
have "special needs," and the idea fit his mission.

"Right away I loved it," Tim said. "I said I wanted to do the event and have it everywhere—all over the country."

Tim spent his early years in the Philippines where his parents were missionaries. There he saw the love his parents had for the people, and the importance of serving others was instilled in his heart.

He said God's salvation gave him the responsibility to give back to others and make a difference in their lives.

When he was 15, Tim visited a remote village and met a boy who was born with his feet backwards. Some thought of the boy as cursed, but Tim showed him the love of Christ and held him.

His passion to help others was born that day. And today, it continues to show through his hallmark Night to Shine annual events that provide an evening dedicated to making thousands of people with special needs feel blessed.

"It's such a part of our identity and our worth about understanding how much God loves us," Tim said. "For us to be able to help this community to where the biggest event in their city and their town is for them to understand their worth. It's not enough that they know that we love them, but the God of this universe loves them."

The first year the Night to Shine was launched, it was held in 44 churches.

In 2019, more than 655 churches participated and helped to give more than 100,000 guests a Night to Shine that involved more than 200,000 volunteers.

"After the first year, it just blew up, and it's so cool," Tim said. "It's such a blessing, and we are grateful to all the churches that help to have an impact on lives. It's my favorite night of the year, and I look forward to it so much. Right after it's over, we start planning for next year. We gather input from all over and make necessary adjustments on how we can improve."

For at least one night a year, the guests get to wear a fancy dress or tuxedo and attend a prom event where they feel like queens and kings for the evening. They have their hair done just right and even have their shoes shined. A dinner is held in their honor, and their entrance into the ballroom is announced to everyone in attendance.

> Because you are precious in my eyes, and honored, and I love you, I give men in return for you, peoples in exchange for your life.
>
> —Isaiah 43:4

Do you make others feel special? What do you do to show attention to those you love?

In the Huddle

It's easy to take your spouse and your children for granted. Maybe you put overtime at the job ahead of them, or your recreational hobbies take priority. Remember that your family is one of God's greatest blessings, and he expects you to nurture them and give them your undivided attention.

Cross the Goal Line

If you have not given your family the priority you should, you can start today. It's not as complicated as you might think. In fact, it's simple. Here are some ways and steps you can do each day to make sure they know where they stand in your life. Make His name shine.

- Spend time each day: Set aside time each day just to talk with your spouse and find out about his or her day. Find out what's important to your kids, what they have been doing at school, and what they would like to do on the weekend. Always appreciate your family's presence and put them before your job or other activities you enjoy.

- Plan special events just for them: You know how it makes you feel when you receive an invitation to an event in the mail. You feel privileged and special. Take the time to plan a special date night just for you and your spouse with no kids involved. Do a sleepover with the kids in a tent out in the backyard. Make your loved ones feel important.

- Be available: Focus on the needs of your family and be a sounding board for them. Share your own experiences and favorite Scriptures to help them through life's questions and tough times. Listen to their problems and pray with them for God's direction in their lives.

- Encourage them: Everyone wants to know that someone believes in them. Be the biggest cheerleader for the goals, ambitions, and desires of your spouse and your children. Allow your kids to fail but be there to help them back up when it happens. Don't fight their battles for them, but show them through Scripture how to depend on God to stand in the gap for them.

Let the wise hear and increase in learning, and the one who understands obtain guidance.

—Proverbs 1:5

The Night to Shine is so massive that it takes thousands of volunteers and thousands of hours to plan and come together to produce this magical night. Make sure you put your primary focus on those who mean the most to you. If you spend time trying to make your co-workers feel special and leave your family out of the picture, shame on you. Next to God, your spouse and kids should be the most important people in your life. Don't take your family for granted and do your best to make them feel special every day.

DAY 18
BE THANKFUL, EVEN WHEN IT'S HARD

Minkah Fitzpatrick
Free Safety
Pittsburgh Steelers

By Del Duduit

Give thanks in all circumstances; for this is the will of God in Christ Jesus for you.

—1 Thessalonians 5:18

Minkah Fitzpatrick grew up in New Jersey and in 2011, his family lost everything to Hurricane Irene.

His father was a truck mechanic and worked hard. Soon after the storm hit, their house was destroyed, and they did not have flood insurance. Within hours, they were homeless.

He, his parents, and three siblings moved into his grandparents' basement and lived there for a year.

Minkah went to Jersey City St. Peter's Preparatory School which was not cheap. His football talents caught the eyes of many college scouts.

But his family struggled financially, and he ate lunch in the "peanut butter" room, which was designed for students who could not afford a regular school lunch. He offered to quit football and go somewhere else to help his parents financially.

He said he felt selfish, but they assured him all would be okay, and they relied on their faith to pull them through.

Four years later, he was on the football field at Alabama, the powerhouse of the SEC. He made it.

His accomplishments speak for themselves.

In 2019, he made the Pro Bowl and was chosen First Team All Pro.

In college, he helped the Crimson Tide to win two national championships and was a Consensus All American in 2016 and 2017. He won the Jim Thorpe Award and was twice selected First Team All-SEC.

The young man can play football, and after only two seasons in the NFL, he has a long career ahead of him.

His experiences and his faith in God have kept him going, especially through the tough times.

"My faith is the reason I play this game," he told me. "God has been faithful to me and my family during the most difficult times in our lives. And now we are reaping the benefits of going through the trial and depending on Him to bring us out."

Minkah had moments when he questioned the Lord's plan in his time of trial. Doubt and confusion will not come from God but is a tool used by the other team. But he made it through and now uses his platform to tell others about his journey. He loves to give God the glory in all he does.

> Rejoice not over me, O my enemy; when I fall, I shall rise; when I sit in darkness, the LORD will be a light to me.
>
> —Micah 7:8

What struggles have you gone through? How did you respond?

In the Huddle

Conflict and personal challenges are a part of life. There's a good chance you will encounter a major obstacle in your life at one time or another. The plans for your future might look bright, but circumstances have a way of storming into your path and interfering with your timeline. Minkah's family lost everything they had in a hurricane at the worst possible time. He had plans of playing football at a high level, and at the time, his hopes were dashed when the storm took their home. What losses have you survived? Have dark clouds of doubt rolled into your life and the winds tossed you about? How have you managed to cope? Are you focused on the storm, or on the One who can bring peace?

Cross the Goal Line

When you are sacked behind the line of scrimmage on three straight downs, you might feel discouraged and want to give up hope. But you still have one down left to try to reach the marker. Life is not fair at times, and you will be faced with decisions you never anticipated having to make. You might have to choose to relocate because of a job loss, or a physician has just laid out a set of options for you to choose regarding treatment options for an ill loved one. You can survive the storm and live to see the sun come up again. Here are some ways to handle the challenges:

- Accept what has happened and don't go into denial: If a tragic event has taken place, you need to acknowledge the facts. This will allow you to move on, and you don't do yourself any favors if you pretend or live in a state of make-believe. Acknowledge that you need help from God, and allow Him to move in your life and provide comfort.

- Seek God in prayer: Think back to a time when you were hurt as a child. Your mother or father usually made you feel better and gave you assurance that all would be okay. The same is true with the Lord. He will reach down and take your hand or hold you, just when you need it the most. His arms of protection will help to give you the peace you need to continue. "He made the storm be still, and the waves of the sea were hushed" (Psalm 107:29).

- Ask for help: Never be too proud to seek counsel or advice. This doesn't mean to open up about your problems to just anyone. But if you have a trusted close friend or pastor who has the best for you in mind, you can confide in them.

- Praise your way through: Whether you have come out of the storm or remain in the swirls, give God praise and honor. Remember that Paul, who had been beaten, shipwrecked, and tossed in prison, thanked the Lord every day. If you can worship Christ in the toughest of trials, He will take care of you and command the winds to obey. "There will be a booth for shade by day from the heat, and for a refuge and a shelter from the storm and rain" (Isaiah 4:6).

- Prepare for victory: The day will arrive when the clouds will roll away and the sun begins to shine. You must exercise patience and trust and wait on God's timetable. If the coach calls your name and puts you in the game, you need to be equipped and not be running around looking for your helmet. Be ready because your moment of victory will arrive. Stay faithful, read your playbook, and work out in prayer every day.

Minkah's trials got him ready to play at Alabama and then go on to the NFL. He went through the fire and flood for a reason. God never left him or his family. You will face battles in life that may be unique. But follow Minkah's lead. Go through it without complaining and adopt a positive outlook.

"It's easy to worship when you are on the mountaintop," Minkah added. "But can you do it when you are in the valley? That's the true testament of faith."

DAY 19
MAKE THE SACRIFICE

Grant Haley
Cornerback
New Orleans Saints

By Del Duduit

The LORD is my shepherd; I shall not want. He makes me to lie down in green pastures; He leads me beside the still waters. He restores my soul; He leads me in the paths of righteousness For His name's sake.
—Psalm 23:1–3 NKJV

Players in the NFL are inspired by their own unique stories. A role model might have helped them along the way, or perhaps they overcame enormous obstacles to reach their goal.

Grant Haley's inspiration came from his mother.

A few years back, Carla was diagnosed with primary sclerosing cholangitis, or PSC, which is a chronic disease that affects the bile ducts. A pediatrician in Atlanta, Georgia and the owner of Genesis Healthcare Associates, she received a liver transplant in 2019.

"We have a close relationship, and she means everything to me," Grant said. "Our entire family is based on Jesus Christ. You can tell that by the name of her practice."

Carla's favorite Scripture is Psalm 23, also dear to Grant's heart.

"Those verses give me strength to go on," he said. "We all go through bad things, and some days you just don't feel it. But I watched how my mom dealt with her situation, and her strength encourages me every day—what she went through and how she never lost hope."

His mother and father raised the family in church and made each of their three children hold true to commitments they made.

They emphasized dedication to family, church, school, and sports. Quitting was never an option, and Grant emboldened his mother's stubborn and feisty attitude.

He credits his mother as the main reason he made it to the NFL.

"I remember her driving me up and down the east coast for football camps and how she took time out of her life for me," he said. "I'm talking about taking me to Florida, North Carolina and Virginia—she really sacrificed for me."

Those memories have instilled in him a desire to do good and to appreciate the sacrifices others have made for him.

"There is so much more in life and things that can affect your family every day," he added. "I have learned to have a positive outlook. I am growing into a man, and people watch me to see how I respond. I have to put forth a good image and live up to that image. People will depend on you whether you have a good day or a bad one. My mom was always positive—always. The outlook she has inspires me."

Surely goodness and mercy shall follow me all the days of
my life; and I will dwell in the house of the LORD, forever.
—Psalm 23:6 NKJV

Who do you put first in your life? Is it yourself? Or do
you make a point to sacrifice so others can live up to their
potential?

In the Huddle

What would you do for your kids? What would you do for
your parents? Have you ever put your life on hold to help
loved ones with their problems? Suppose you had to meet
with a client after hours to close a deal, and it was the same
night that your son had an important game. What would
you do? Or maybe you promised your daughter you would
take her shopping, and then you received an invitation to
do something fun with your friends.

Cross the Goal Line

What lengths will you go to put the needs of others ahead
of your own? There is a difference in doing what you want
to do, and doing what you must do. How do you prioritize?
Are you selfish or giving? There is nothing wrong with a little "me time," but you must meet your obligations. Here are
some ways to put the feelings of others in front of your own.

- Be compassionate: Ask God to teach you how to care
  about the needs of others. We are all inclined to put
  ourselves first, but God can give you the kind soul that

you need to devote more time to your loved ones. Ask Him to change your heart so you can see the needs of those who may not be as blessed as you. He can make you a giving and thoughtful person and open doors for you to be a light to others. "But He, being full of compassion, forgave their iniquity, and did not destroy them. Yes, many a time He turned His anger away, and did not stir up all His wrath" (Psalm 78:38 NKJV).

- Empathize: This is close to the first point, but there is a difference. When you are empathetic, you consider the needs of those around you, and you put yourself in their shoes to try to understand their situations better. Think of how you would feel if you were in their situation and how you would want people to treat you. Ask God to open your eyes and show you how to be the hands and feet of Jesus.

- Demonstrate a servant's heart: Once God shows you how He wants you to care for others, put what He reveals to you into action. The Holy Spirit might impress you to donate time and money to a worthy cause. Show God's love to all despite their situation, and refrain from judging them. One day, You could be just like them and may need help yourself. "As each one has received a gift, minister it to one another, as good stewards of the manifold grace of God" (1 Peter 4:10 NKJV).

- Give God the glory: Helping others is an opportunity for you to serve God and spread the gospel. You should not strive for public attention for the work you do. If you snap selfies while working a soup line and post them on Facebook, you must ask yourself: Am I doing this for the right reason? Is my goal to make quality of life better for others or to make myself look good? If your goal is to impress others, you are in the wrong business. Put others' needs in front of your own with humility, and don't expect anything in return. When you learn to sacrifice for the sake of others and for no other reason, you are following God's heart.

Carla did not haul her son all over the east coast for her own glory. She took time off work because she knew it was important to her son. She did it for the right reasons. And in the midst of it all, she epitomized the love of God. She gave of herself so her son could reach his dream.

DAY 20
GOD HAS PLANS

Tim Tebow
Quarterback, Retired
New York Jets

By Del Duduit

Many are the plans in the mind of a man, but it is the purpose of the LORD that will stand.

—Proverbs 19:21

Tim Tebow is an extraordinary athlete with some amazing accomplishments.

When he was quarterback at the University of Florida, he led the Gators to two BCS National Championships and two conference titles. Named the Associated Press Player of the Year in 2007, he won the Maxwell Award twice, the *Sporting News* Player of the Year Award, and the prestigious Heisman Trophy, just to name a few. This was pretty good for a kid who was born in the Philippines while his parents served as missionaries.

Although he was a decorated college football player, his first love was baseball.

"When I was four, my parents signed me up for the White Sox at Normandy Baseball Park," he said. "I picked number 35 just like Frank Thomas—that was my number and I loved it."

Throughout his life, he wanted to play on the diamond, but his best route to a college education was on the gridiron.

Head Coach Urban Meyer recruited him, and his mom was in favor of the choice, so he opted to throw the pigskin instead of the baseball.

"I love football too," he said. "And it was hard to pass up. We even talked about if I could play both."

Florida had just won the National Championship and Tim had captured the Heisman when he approached his football coach about playing baseball.

"He was supportive, but I didn't want to take away from what I was doing with the team, but at the same time, I wanted to chase my dream," he said. "That football team was awesome."

In 2010, Tim was taken in the first round in the NFL draft by the Denver Broncos.

On January 8, 2012 God used Tebow in an amazing way to tell the world about John 3:16. "For God so loved the world, that he gave his only Son, that whoever believes in him should not perish but have eternal life."

Tebow played his most memorable game when the Broncos hosted Pittsburgh in the first round of the NFL playoffs. He threw for 316 yards, which included an 80-yard touchdown pass to Demaryius Thomas on the first play of overtime to win the contest. For that game he set a league record with a 31.6-yard-per-pass average. And to top it off, the fourth quarter television ratings came in at 31.6.

Coincidence all the stats related to John 3:16? No. Obvious message? Yes.

While in Denver, Tim became friends with some members of the Colorado Rockies, and the baseball bug bit him again.

However, when the next season rolled around, he found himself on the roster of the New York Jets. After a disappointing tenure with the new team, he was released.

He met with his agents in the Big Apple and told them he wanted to play baseball.

"All I heard was crickets," Tim said. "I told them that was what I was passionate about."

Within a short time, Tim made the squad of a minor team for the New York Mets organization.

"Both sports are different," he said. "In football, there are moments when you have to 'will it' to happen, and in baseball there is a grind and mental toughness."

Tim has played professional football and baseball well. Although he never saw the success on the diamond that he say on the gridiron, he was grateful for the opportunity to chase his dream.

As a result of his popularity with the fans, he has been able to make an impact on fans who want to come out and see him play.

Although his performance at the pro level has not been what he wanted, there are other reasons that make him smile. His celebrity status is remarkable.

"I try not to let it get in the way because I play and compete," he said. "There are pros and cons. I have to answer more questions from the media and have demands on my time, but then I get to see kids in the hospital who want to see me, and I have the opportunity to make them smile. Without the platform, none of that would be possible, so I'm grateful that I have the chance to make someone feel special."

> Do your best to present yourself to God as one approved, a worker who has no need to be ashamed, rightly handling the word of truth.
>
> —2 Timothy 2:15

In the Huddle

Do people want to spend time with you? Are you a positive influence on others no matter what has gone wrong in your life? You can control your effort and your attitude no matter what obstacles come your way. While Tim spent little time in the NFL and has never made it to the major leagues, he is revered by many people who look to him as a positive influence and a great ambassador for Christ. His message of hope makes other want to be around him. What kind of signal do you send out to others?

Cross the Goal Line

Don't publicize your problems to everyone you meet, or they will begin to avoid you whenever they see you. Everything will not always go your way, but give your heartaches and disappointments to God, and confide in your spouse, pastor, or close Christian friends. But don't dump your troubles on those around you. Make the effort to share the

Lord's good news and joy with others. You don't have to be the life of the party when you are dealing with life's issues, but at the same time you don't want to bring others down with you. Stay close to God, pray and read His word daily, and He will help you to trust Him and to show the love of God in your heart to others. Here are some more ways to brighten up the atmosphere:

- Be positive: There are many times in our lives when we don't receive something we prayed for from God, but we realize later that it was due to His protection and ability to see the big picture. He may very well have a better story for your life than you could have ever imagined. Focus on the positive, ask God to keep you out of the dumps, and trust Him for your future. Encourage your friends to look for the bright side when bad news comes their way and to depend on God for His mercy and grace. "A joyful heart is good medicine, but a crushed spirit dries up the bones" (Proverbs 17:22).

- Be honest: Don't ever tell fibs or bend the truth. One lie grows into bigger lies, and your family and friends will lose trust in you. If you are asked for your opinion, share it in love and be open to listening to the ideas of ideas. This may open the door for you to witness to them about God's love.

- Be involved: Volunteer your time in youth sports or at your kids' school. Lift them up and encourage them to do their best, and keep your complaints to yourself. Find a way to compliment your spouse, family, and co-workers every day. A few words of inspiration and praise can go a long way to boost the spirits of those around you.

- Be hopeful: Expect good things from the Lord and count your blessings each day. Be optimistic that He can take anything bad and turn it into good for His glory. Support the dreams and visions of others, and pray for them to trust God and never doubt that His plan is best. "But if we hope for what we do not see, we wait for it with patience" (Romans 8:25).

- Be blessed: People are attracted to those who smile and have joy. You can still do this even though problems arise. You are a child of the King and have every reason to have peace in your heart. Put a contagious smile on your face to be a blessing to others. "Blessed is the man who trusts in the LORD, whose trust is the LORD" (Jeremiah 17:7).

Tim makes people feel good because he carries a message of hope. People are drawn to him because he shows the love of God. Today, Tim always attracted a large audience when he played baseball, but they were mostly attracted to him for his positive outlook on life and his encouraging witness to others. He has a smile that only God can give, and he provides a shining example of what it's like to have joy and peace in your heart to people around the country.

DAY 21
AGE IS JUST A NUMBER

Adam Vinatieri
Kicker
Indianapolis Colts

By Michelle Medlock-Adams

But those who trust in the LORD will find new strength.
They will soar high on wings like eagles. They will run and
not grow weary. They will walk and not faint.
—Isaiah 40:31 NLT

Indianapolis Colts kicker Adam Vinatieri can now say
something few other NFL players have ever been able
to say—that many of his fellow Colts were born *after* he
played his first NFL game.

Turning forty-six during the 2018 season, Adam is defi-
nitely one of the oldest players to still compete in the NFL.
He is a proud member of the "Over Forty Club," which
boasts of more than sixty players who currently play or
have played in the NFL at the age of forty or older.

And Adam isn't thinking of hanging up his cleats any
time soon. He told Colts.com that he loves playing today
as much as he did when he began his NFL career in 1996.
And according to statistics, he's getting better all the time.
In 2017, he made twenty-nine of thirty-four field goals

(85.3 percent), which is a little higher than his career average of 84.3 percent.

When he gets up to kick, fans can head for the concessions stand with no worries because it's pretty much a sure thing—the kick will be good.

By the end of the 2018 season, Adam became the number-one scorer in NFL history. That record was held by Morten Andersen, who held the top spot since he retired in 2007.

Fans and critics alike have said Vinatieri is aging like a fine wine, and Vinatieri plans to keep it that way for as long as possible. He still has dreams and goals to accomplish, and as long as he can remain healthy, he plans to keep on kicking.

If we're being honest, I bet all of us have dreams we've never realized but here's the good news—it's not too late! No matter your age, you're not too old to fulfill the plans God has for your life. The parade hasn't passed you by. You haven't missed the boat. You're not too old!

Did you know legendary folk artist Grandma Moses did not start painting until she was seventy-six years old? Without any art classes or special training, she painted simple, realistic pictures of rural settings—paintings that are of historic importance.

Look at Sarah in the Bible. She didn't have her son of promise—Isaac—until she was very old. Sarah had given up on having her own child, but God hadn't given up on fulfilling her dream and using her to bring Isaac into the world.

So, what dream has God placed on the inside of you? Is it to write a book? Is it to teach a Bible study? Is it to start your own business? Now let me ask you this—what is holding you back? According to Jeremiah 29:11, God has a good plan for your life. He hasn't forgotten about it, and you shouldn't either.

> I can do all things through Christ who strengthens me.
> —Philippians 4:13 NKJV

In the Huddle

No matter how old you are, what you've been through, or what you're going through right now, God has a plan, a purpose, and a perfect peace just waiting for you. It's not too late, and you're not too old. God's timing is always perfect, and this is His time. This is His time to work through you to accomplish great and mighty things! So, be excited! God isn't through with us yet, and His Word says He will renew our strength. We will run and not grow weary! So, lace up those shoes! Run your race! I'll run mine, and we'll finish strong together.

Cross the Goal Line

Have you ever felt like you're too old or too short or too heavy or too _____ to accomplish your dreams? Take a note from Adam's playbook and press on toward your goals.

• Don't let the naysayers deter you.

- Don't let your age or anything else stop you from dreaming big and going for those dreams.
- Define your dreams and develop goals to reach them.
- Pray over those dreams and goals every day.

The Bible says to "write the vision and make it plain" (Habakkuk 2:2), so why not create a vision board? Place pictures on it that represent your dreams and goals and display it prominently in your house so you can be reminded daily. God placed those dreams on your heart. Pursue them with faith and perseverance.

DAY 22
WHERE IDENTITY LIES

Mark Sanchez
Quarterback
Chicago Bears

By Ryan Farr

> I have been crucified with Christ and I no longer live, but Christ lives in me. The life I now live in the body, I live by faith in the Son of God, who loved me and gave himself for me.
>
> —Galatians 2:20 NIV

Playing in the NFL is the dream of every young kid who steps out on an old plot of green grass on a weekend afternoon to imitate their favorite Sunday warrior. Wearing helmets twice the size of their head with replica jerseys donning the number of their favorite players, these youngsters look forward to one day being able to do the impossible on the gridiron.

Later in life, however, the reality sets in that few players will ever make it to that big-league paradise. Somewhere along the line, those young athletes put aside their plastic helmets and begin to focus on new careers. Some will be accountants and business owners. Others will be teachers or grocery store managers. While far from their childhood hopes, these vocations begin to become what they are about and what they are known for; they become a part of their identity. While it is never a bad thing to enjoy your work, there is a certain danger in that job being the central focus of your life.

Just ask one of those youngsters that is living his big-league dream: Mark Sanchez. And just like any other job, the life of an NFL quarterback is a constant struggle of where to find and draw identity.

"My relationship with God is the most important thing," says Mark, "regardless of your profession or what you do in your day-to-day life." It is easy to get caught up in productivity numbers, the amount clients are paying you for a job, or the stat line after an NFL game. The danger in this is that life and work are typically a roller coaster of peaks and valleys. Sanchez is no stranger to that challenge, having been all the way on the top as a first-round draft pick and eventual NFL starter, all the way to a free agent fighting to make a roster.

"[A relationship with God] keeps you grounded," he says, "because there is always something bigger and more important than you or your struggles." Making that realization is what has made Mark a stronger person; being able to keep perspective in times of earth's struggle.

Because when it comes down to it, earthly success is not important to God. The Lord has a plan for each of our lives, and part of that plan is to glorify Him and point to Him in everyday life. Some may ask, "How could my profession possibly be important to God?" Consider what Colossians 3:23 says, "Whatever you do, work at it with all your heart, as working for the Lord, not for human masters."

Whether you're a professional quarterback or sitting behind an office desk, consider today how you will honor God in your workplace.

> Therefore, if anyone is in Christ, the new creation has come. The old has gone, the new is here.
> —2 Corinthians 5:17 NIV

In the Huddle

In hearing Mark Sanchez's challenge to keep your relationship with God a central focus in your life, have you felt challenged by the state of your own relationship with a God who has bigger plans than earthly success for your life? Take some time to think about the work you do, the people you interact with, and the opportunities you have to be a living example of Jesus Christ each day. Then make a game plan for how you can use those opportunities to gain a bigger perspective. Decide on one way you can show Christ today and then go and do it!

Cross the Goal Line

As you consider that challenge, it is important to contemplate what Galatians 2:20 tells us about our lives as followers of God. Because there are some necessary changes that take place when we turn our lives over to Him. Ponder this …

- It says you no longer live: Seems pretty morbid, right? But if you step back and take a look at this statement and consider its meaning, what a freeing verse! We no longer operate like the rest of the world, and suddenly the rat race of industry success means less and less.

- Christ lives in you: And it keeps getting better! Not only have you died to sin and the old way of doing things, but God has given you a whole new perspective and a mission that He is placing you on. But He doesn't send you on by yourself. God promises to be with us and guide us as we maneuver His will for our lives.

- We live by faith: Do you remember a time where you had a big project due at work and it was all you could think about? The one that kept you working through the night and into the morning hours to ensure it was completed. Well guess what? That doesn't end! Because as we pursue God's will we still need to, well, work! But instead of placing all of our anxiety on our own human weakness, we know we can rely on a God bigger than our deadlines and bigger than our problems. Is there something you need to surrender to Him today?

- We realize the message of the gospel: There is one thing that should never leave our minds and always give us joy (remember joy and happiness are not the same thing) no matter what the situation: the fact Christ gave His life for us to have life. He died and rose again to defeat the grave and free us from sin. You will have down times in your job and in life, but this truth should always give us comfort.

- The possibilities are endless: You are on a new mission now. And it has nothing to do with a bigger house, a nicer car, or more stuff. It's about seeing people brought into a relationship with a God who loves them dearly.

Make no mistake, there's work to be done. But it's time to stop seeing our jobs as the thing that gives us identity and instead see them as mission fields where God's transforming power in our lives can show through. Today's challenge is to write Galatians 2:20 on a sticky note or index card and place it somewhere visible in your office to always remember the real work God has given you to do for His glory.

DAY 23
PRIORITIES

Vernon Fox
NFL Veteran and Christian Speaker

By Beckie Lindsey

Jesus replied: "'Love the Lord your God with all your heart and with all your soul and with all your mind.'"
—Matthew 22:37 NIV

We all have priorities—things that are most important to us. They inspire our behavior and influence our decision-making in life. Some priorities are good and some ... not so good. Perhaps you've heard someone tell another person, *your priorities are out of balance.*

It happens even to the best of us.

German writer Johann Wolfgang von Goethe grasped the importance of priorities when he said, "Things which matter most must never be at the mercy of things which matter least."

Veteran NFL player Vernon Fox has his priorities in order. In fact, his profile on Outreach.com's speaker network webpage states, "Vernon embodies a man with proper priorities: Faith, Family, and Career. Vernon has served in ministry for over ten years and in the capacity of a minister since 2008."

But it wasn't always that way. Although raised in a Christian home, Vernon reached a point in his early college years when he wanted to explore life without what he viewed at the time as *restrictions*. He started living his own way without consulting God. It wasn't long before God got his attention through a unique friendship established in his freshman year.

"This guy was my age and a virgin. He was in a committed relationship but remained pure. The choices he made were ones I thought only adults could do. We made a strong connection and at the age of 18, I recommitted my life to Christ. It was personal. It was my own conscious decision to live for Christ."

Vernon said making this decision was a turning point in his life. His purpose was bigger. He was called to be set apart and different. For the first time, *Christ* was first and Fox was confident that all the other things in his life would fall into place.

"All that I am, the opportunities afforded me—everything has come by way of my commitment first to God. There is no me without God. My relationship with God is essential and that's what I want everyone I meet to know."

Are your priorities evident to those around you? Would others see Christ as your number one priority?

But seek first his kingdom and his righteousness, and all these things will be given to you as well.
—Matthew 6:33 NIV

In the Huddle

Let's face it, life is complicated and we all have many things to balance. Vernon strives to keep it simple by remembering: Faith, Family, and, Career.

1. Faith: Growing in his relationship to God remains Fox's daily commitment and number-one priority.
2. Family: When Vernon got married to his wife Tai, his family also became a priority. The family of God is equally important, which means regular church attendance and service.
3. Career: After retiring from the NFL, Vernon became an inspirational speaker. Fox has shared his story of faith at schools, churches, and organizations while also coaching high school football. It is important to Vernon that his students and other coaches see him as a man of faith with Jesus at the center of his life.

Cross the Goal Line

To get our priorities in proper balance, we must first take a look at where and how we are spending our time. This shouldn't be a one-time event. Because our lives are constantly changing, it is recommended to reevaluate priorities on a yearly basis. If something of significance, such as an illness, job loss, or a birth occurs, a reevaluation may need to come sooner. The way we live our day-to-day lives is a good indication of where our priorities lie.

Following are questions that will help shed some light on your priorities. After answering them, ask a trusted friend or family member to answer the questions *about* you.

The Priorities Test
What do you think about the most?
Where does your money go first?
How do you spend your time?
List your top five priorities.

Once you've answered the questions and received the list back from your family member or friend, it's time to evaluate.

If things are not in proper balance, the first place to start is prayer. Ask God to help you get your priorities right.

In John 10:10 (NLT), Jesus said, "My purpose is to give them a rich and satisfying life." The key to having this rich and satisfying life is to keep God in His rightful place in our priorities. God said to Abraham, "Walk [habitually] before Me" (Genesis 17:1 AMP).

Notice God instructed Abraham to be *habitual* in walking with Him and living for Him. We can do this by establishing daily habits of prayer, worship, and time in the Word.

Here's the hitch: God doesn't *only* want to be at the top of our to-do list. He wants to be the *center* of everything in our lives. This is why He said we must love Him with all we are.

Friends, the Christian life is a process. When you were a baby, did you just get up and walk? Of course not. It was a process. Even when you started walking, it was clumsy and you often fell down. The goal is regular growth.

Most of us realize God should be our top priority, however seeking God first is easier said than done. The good news is, God wants to help. He knows our weaknesses and what distract us. Even when we are unfaithful, He is still faithful to us. He is waiting for us to ask for His help.

When God is the center our daily lives, the by-product is what Jesus promises to give us, "a rich and satisfying life." Of course, it won't be perfect or without troubles. But a life lived for God's purpose is one of fulfillment and balance of priorities. This way, when crossing the goal line in heaven, we will hear these words, "Well done, good and faithful servant!" (Matthew 25:23).

DAY 24
THERE IS PEACE

Clinton McDonald
Defensive End
Oakland Raiders

By Cyle Young

> What, then, shall we say in response to these things? If God
> is for us, who can be against us?
> —Romans 8:31 NIV

Defensive end Clinton McDonald started his spiritual journey at the age of ten. Back in those days, when he read the
Bible he would often come across a word he didn't understand, so he would look those words up in a dictionary.
And as he struggled to navigate the sometimes-difficult
translation, he learned all about God's peace. Especially
with stories about historical Bible characters like David
and Saul. After David fled from Saul, Saul pursued him
relentlessly. But even while he was on the run for his life,
God gave David a perfect peace. He kept David in the
center of His will.

Clinton had never truly experienced God's peace until a
car accident sent him tumbling and flipping. Laying in the
fetal position amongst broken metal and glass, God gave
Clinton a powerful sense of peace. Everything was going

to be okay, because God was in control. The God of David offered the same sense of peace to a college football player in Memphis, Tennessee. Personally experiencing God's peace for the first time shaped Clinton's mind and allowed him to see Christ in a new light. Every time Clinton would feel defeated or get down on himself, he would remember the promises of Scripture.

> Do not let your hearts be troubled. You believe in God; believe also in me.
>
> —John 14:1 NIV

When fear or doubt sets in, Clinton thinks back on the word of John 4. He recognizes that Jesus offers him the same peace David experienced. Jesus conquered all sin and death, and with Christ's help, we not only overcome our difficulties but also experience God's true peace.

> No, in all these things we are more than conquerors through him who loved us.
>
> —Romans 8:37 NIV

God's peace got Clinton through the difficulty he experienced in 2013 when the Seattle Seahawks cut him from the team. He shared about that moment, "God consumed me with perfect peace." McDonald stayed faithful to God, and God in turn revealed a much bigger plan. Clinton rejoined the team and later went on to win the Super Bowl with the Seattle Seahawks. But he couldn't have done it without God's everlasting peace.

In the Huddle

Have you ever experienced God's peace like Clinton McDonald has? In difficult moments you need to double down with God and His Word. Most people's initial reaction to setbacks or challenges is to fear and worry, but there is a better way. Devote yourself to growing closer to Christ. Get into God's Word and allow God to give you a peace that surpasses all human understanding.

Cross the Goal Line

Peace is something you experience, but it is also a person—Jesus Christ. If you want to know peace, you have to know Jesus as Savior and Lord of your life. Whatever troubles life throws at you can be conquered, and you can endure through it if you allow God to fill you with his peace. "Peace I leave with you; my peace I give you. I do not give to you as the world gives. Do not let your hearts be troubled and do not be afraid" (John 14:27 NIV).

- Get in the Word: Right before Clinton had been cut from the Seahawks, God impressed on him more than ever that he needed to get in the Word. The Holy Spirit had been convicting him to get more involved with studying and reading the Bible. And he did, and God's Word sustained him through his departure from the team and allowed him to rejoice even more when he later rejoined the Seahawks. You also need to get in the Word. Devote time in your day to interacting with the Bible; it's your guidebook for a spiritually fulfilling life, and it prepares you for handling all of life trials, good and bad. "All Scripture is God-breathed and is useful for teaching, rebuking, correcting and training in righteousness" (2 Timothy 3:16 NIV).

- Acknowledge Jesus: The Bible calls Jesus Christ the "Prince of Peace." This title wasn't given by accident. It wasn't a mistake. Jesus is a bringer of peace to a broken and sinful world. By acknowledging Jesus Christ as Savior of the world, you elevate Him to the rightful place as ruler of your heart and you accept the peace He brings to all those who call him Lord. "For to us a child is born, to us a son is given, and the government will be on his shoulders. And he will be called Wonderful Counselor, Mighty God, Everlasting Father, Prince of Peace" (Isaiah 9:6 NIV).

- Embrace Peace: Not only do you need to acknowledge the Prince of Peace, but you also want to embrace the understanding of the state of peace. Peace can transcend all the good and bad of life. It is a state of knowing your place in the world and accepting once and for all that God is in control. When you actively attempt to choose peace in your daily routine and also in difficult moments, you discover that life is more fulfilling. In so doing, you can cast off worry, anxiety, and fear that often holds most people back from experiencing true joy. "Therefore, since we have been justified through faith, we have peace with God through our Lord Jesus Christ" (Romans 5:1 NIV).

Peace is a promise. Thousands of years ago, God promised to send peace into the world through His Son Jesus. He fulfilled that promise and continues to allow His followers to know and understand personal peace with the help of the Holy Spirit. You can know peace too. When your trust is placed in Jesus Christ, you will be able to mentally and spiritually overcome any trial that comes your way. You may not always experience the success of winning a Super Bowl like Clinton McDonald, but you will for sure understand the same peace that God allows Clinton to know every time doubt and fear creep into his mind—an everlasting and unsurpassed peace!

DAY 25
BE READY TO SHINE

Jim Kelly
Hall of Fame Quarterback
Buffalo Bills

By Scott McCausey

Therefore, with minds that are alert and fully sober, set
your hope on the grace to be brought to you when Jesus
Christ is revealed at his coming.

—1 Peter 1:13 NIV

Jim Kelly dreamed of walking through the tunnel of Beaver
Stadium with 100,000 screaming fans welcoming the Nittany Lions. He grew up a fan of the program and attended
their football camps his junior and senior year of high
school, hoping to make his dream a reality.

But as his senior year ended and the High School
National Signing Date was a day away, the Pennsylvania
State University coach shared sad news. "Jim, I just want
to let you know we already signed two All-State quarter-
backs. We'd like to offer you a full scholarship, but as a
linebacker."

"Linebacker?" He wasn't made for linebacker; he was a
quarterback. So he chose to play for the Miami Hurricanes
and Coach Howard Schnellenberger. They promised him a

chance to start, but Jim quickly found college football very competitive, and was relegated to fourth string, earning him a red-shirt (a term given to a player who is granted an extra year of eligibility while only practicing with the team for his first season.)

About halfway through his red-shirt season, Miami traveled to face number nineteen-ranked Penn State. Since Jim was still a backup, a trip home to see his parents and be treated to chocolate chip cookies and fresh clothes was the peak of his excitement. But just a couple hours before the game, Coach Shnellenberger gave him the news. "I decided to give you your big chance, you're starting at quarterback today. You've earned this opportunity."

Jim replied shockingly, "Excuse me?" He dashed for the nearest bathroom and threw up for twenty minutes. He was about to start against the team that told him he wasn't good enough to be their quarterback.

> So you also must be ready, because the Son of Mam will come at an hour when you do no expect him.
> —Matthew 24:44 NIV

In the Huddle

Preparing for what is in store is not always easy, but generally we have time to commit for the upcoming challenge. If it's a big test, we can pour hours into study. If there's a make-or-break project at work, we dedicate efforts to exceed expectations. But what of those times when a situation is tossed in our laps and we are counted on to get the job done? Are you ready when trouble hits?

Cross the Goal Line

Constructing ourselves takes effort and sometimes hurts because we must get outside our comfort zones. God tells us we should be ready in all circumstances. "But concerning that day and hour no one knows, not even the angels of heaven, nor the Son, but the Father only" (Matthew 24:36).

Oftentimes we've already done the preparation work, we just have to get our minds ready for action. In Jim's case, he'd played football his entire life. He'd practiced with the team, studied the plays, and knew the game plan. He was trained for a time such as this. That doesn't mean it's easy, but it does mean we are given skills to accomplish tasks. Here's some practical applications when we find ourselves thrust in the limelight.

- Pray: Often one of the most overlooked things in our lives is to give our problem to God. He not only tells us we can do this, but He invites us. "Trust in the LORD with all your heart, and do not lean on your own understanding. In all your ways acknowledge him, and he will make straight your paths" (Proverbs 3:5–6). When we ask our Heavenly Father to help guide our actions, we can receive a sense of peace to deliver us from our troubles.

- Don't Worry: Yes, this is so much easier said than done. But what is gained from worrying about the outcome? When we trust in the Lord with an understanding that he already has won the day, worry is shed from our hearts and minds. "Humble yourselves, therefore, under the mighty hand of God so that at the proper time he may exalt you, casting all your anxieties on him, because he cares for you" (1 Peter 5:6–7). You can also trust in the skills and abilities God has blessed you and let those skills take over.

- Understanding the Perspective: We train our entire lives to excel when called upon. What we often forget is our light is a reflection of Jesus Christ in our actions. Those same actions dictate a servant's heart, showing what and who we believe. There's great opportunity through this platform to advance God's kingdom, showing love when the pressure is at the highest point. "I will instruct you and teach you in the way you should go; I will counsel you with my eye upon you" (Psalm 32:8).

- Be Ready to Lead: God gave Noah instructions to build a grand ark. Included were the blueprints and details of who the passengers were going to be. There was no surprise a huge storm was brewing, but Noah knew what he had to do. We should all be ready for action when the time arises; this will bring confidence. "The fear of the LORD is the beginning of knowledge; fools despise wisdom and instruction" (Proverbs 1:7).

- Know Your Craft: The blood, sweat, and tears you pour into your passion are not for nothing. When you are thrust in the limelight, it is not someone else's moment. Allow your disciplined training to take over and perform to your abilities. "But blessed is the one who trusts in the LORD, whose confidence is in him" (Jeremiah 17:7 NIV).

Jim took the field and threw his first touchdown pass, an eight-yard fade to Jim Joiner. The Hurricanes would never look back and defeated the Nittany Lions 26–10. Jim finished the game an impressive 18 for 31 and three touchdowns. He completed a solid college career and excelled to become a Pro Football Hall of Fame quarterback. You can be a hall of famer in your field and for the kingdom of God. Be ready for the moment to shine your light.

DAY 26
DON'T STUMBLE

Kurt Warner
Hall of Fame Quarterback
St. Louis Rams and Arizona Cardinals

By Del Duduit

> Therefore let us not pass judgment on one another any longer, but rather decide never to put a stumbling block or hindrance in the way of a brother.
>
> —Romans 14:13

Over his remarkable career, Kurt Warner set high standards for other players and men of God. On the field, his accomplishments demand respect and admiration.

He helped guide the St. Louis Rams to a victory in Super Bowl XXXIV for which he also earned MVP honors. He was a four-time Pro-Bowl selection and a two-time NFL MVP winner. In 2008, he won the prestigious Walter Payton NFL Man of the Year Award and in 2001, he was the league passing leader.

In 1999 and 2001, he led the NFL in passing touchdowns and was the passer rating leader. He is also a member of the Arizona Cardinals Ring of Honor, and he is the only player inducted into both the NFL and Arena Football Hall of Fames.

Kurt served as the field general of his teams, and he led them by example. He refused to get in the way of his team's success.

He played with several different personalities and for a number of different coaches. Yet his performance stayed at the top of the league for many years.

The former signal caller acknowledges that players are faced with stumbling blocks each day in the NFL, such as temptations, too much money, and too much free time. "When you are faced with a situation or opportunities you get in the NFL, there is always a wrestling match of, 'Do I take advantage of this, or do I want to represent that?'" he said. "How do I balance the two? Or if I'm not outspoken enough, then I can dabble in things that are right there on that gray line."

These obstacles can come in several forms. But you have to take a stand early in order to be strong. "You know, I learned quickly to be outspoken on things because the more you are, the more it forces you to do what's right," he said. "Because if I told everyone I'm going to represent Jesus, then I'd better do it right. I have an obligation."

Many events can happen in a person's life to make them a hindrance to other Christians.

Over the years there have been scandals and an overemphasis placed on money and the lavish lifestyles led by some televangelists and mega-church pastors. Some churches have split over titles and doctrine and have placed a high priority on social activities rather than on soul-winning.

"I just wish everyone could love one another more and not focus on differences that can form a wedge between us," he said. "We need to focus on our similarities and embrace our differences. There has been too much hatred and ugliness that has come between the vision to see people saved. I wish I could solve that problem, so we could get back to promoting Jesus."

> Therefore, if food makes my brother stumble, I will never again eat meat, lest I make my brother stumble.
> —1 Corinthians 8:13 NKJV

In the Huddle

Have you done something in the past as a follower of Christ that left a negative impact on a person's perception of what a Christian should be? No one is perfect, and we all make mistakes. Perhaps you have shared an off-color joke or a "fisherman's tale" at work that grew bigger each time you told it. Perhaps your coworkers have heard you talk about not drinking or smoking and later saw you at a bar or light one up at a ball game. You might have a lot of money, but you don't help those in need and donate to a charity. Or maybe you gossip around the water cooler instead of talk about the goodness of the Lord. There are many ways you can discourage others from following Jesus.

Cross the Goal Line

You are human and will falter at times. But always be aware that people watch you and who you represent. When you proclaim the Lord as your Savior, you put everyone on notice that you are supposed to be a good example. This is why Kurt advocates an early public confession to set the tone. This puts all who know you on notice that you are different. Here are some ways you can make that statement of faith and hold true to your obligation to be a positive influence and ambassador for Christ:

- Be truthful: If you are placed in a situation where telling the truth might have negative consequences, tell it anyway. No good comes from a lie. Now, this doesn't mean you tell your wife she doesn't look good in a certain dress, but you will know the difference. "The lips of the righteous know what is acceptable, but the mouth of the wicked, what is perverse" (Proverbs 10:32).

- Be positive: No one likes to be around a negative person all the time. Show an outlook of encouragement to others. When you share your testimony, tell of the wonderful life you live because of the Master. You may have problems, but now you have a way to deal with them in a more effective way. Declare His goodness and strive to display an upbeat attitude. "Whatever you do, work heartily, as for the Lord and not for men" (Colossians 3:23).

- Be helpful: When you see a person in need, don't think twice. Lend a hand, and it will not go unnoticed. Don't make a point to brag, but always have a desire to please your heavenly Father first.

- Be dependable: When you make a commitment, show up for practice. Attend church on a regular basis and become involved in Bible studies or church activities. A good player puts in the time and prepares for game day. You are no different as a follower of the Lord.

- Be of service: When you give your time and energy for the Lord, you will receive blessings from above. Kurt put in the time and dedicated a large part of his life to football. He played hard and approached his craft with the right attitude. This is why he is in two halls of fame. When you make the decision to follow Christ, you must have the same mindset. You will not improve your spiritual life unless you read the Bible, pray, and attend church. Offer yourself up to help others around you. For example, you can volunteer at a boy's club or the Salvation Army. Give back and be of service to those less fortunate. You will grow as a follower and inspire others to do similar acts. "If I then, your Lord and Teacher, have washed your feet, you also ought to wash one another's feet" (John 13:14).

Kurt had an impressive impact on his football teams. The championship ring and all the accolades he has received represent this well. But he is even more determined to be an effective witness for his Lord. When you give your life to Christ, you become an instant starter on His team. Stick to the fundamentals, and tear down the barricades in your life.

DAY 27
WHAT DEFINES YOU?

Noah Herron
Running Back
Green Bay Packers

By Scott McCausey

Then [Jesus] said to them, "But who do you say that I am?"
And Peter answered, "The Christ of God."

—Luke 9:20

Noah Herron's time to shine had arrived. After a successful 2006 Green Bay Packers campaign in which he finished the season with a 4.1-yard-per-carry average and caught 29 passes from MVP quarterback Brett Favre, he was poised to be the 2008 starter.

"There was a battle for the starting position, and it was a battle I was able to win," he said. "The pre-season went well for me, and for the first game at least, I was named the starter."

The final game of the preseason had arrived, and Noah played the first quarter with the first string. The Packers were driving against the Tennessee Titans when Favre connected with Noah in the end zone for a six-yard touchdown. This would cement his position, or would it? Noah couldn't get up and stayed on the turf in pain. He sprained his knee.

"This ended my 2007 campaign," he said. "I thought it would be my breakout year and lead to a big second contract."

Instead, this would prove to be the beginning of the end of Noah's NFL career.

> Now you are the body of Christ and individually members of it.
>
> —1 Corinthians 12:27 ESV

In the Huddle

Does success or failure define your identity? When someone hears your name, what comes to their mind? Who do your friends and family say you are? While Noah may be known as a Packer or NFL player, football left him with injuries and "what ifs" he must cope with forever. The cost of a label tattoos his health, yet his passion remains in Christ. Our skill at work or God-given gift should not be the first thing synonymous with your name. The real question is, do you represent Jesus Christ while your gifts are on display?

Cross the Goal Line

Some football players are known by their end zone antics. While these short dances are supposed to be simple celebrations of a touchdown, often they represent something else. They sometimes taunt opposing teams or use this time to represent a political position, all of which incur penalties, costing their team precious yards and sometimes victories. However, the cost of a silly dance also sheds light on the identity of players. This doesn't only happen after touchdowns, it can happen during interviews or even before the game. The following are examples of touchdown celebrations that exemplify players. What do you exemplify through your actions?

- Hand the ball to officials: There was none better than Barry Sanders when it came to classy touchdowns. Whether he scored a game winner or a blowout score, Barry looked for an official and handed him the ball. This exemplifies a level of humbleness not seen in the NFL and is remembered by football fans around the world. "Humble yourselves, therefore, under the mighty hand of God so that at the proper time he may exalt you, casting all your anxieties on him, because he cares for you" (1 Peter 5:6–7). When we humble ourselves to the Father, our actions display our hearts.

- Get Back to Work: While some players go crazy, Super Bowl MVP Nick Foles simply gets back to work. He shakes a few hands and heads to the sideline. This doesn't mean we shouldn't celebrate success but displays how to take it in stride. There's always another challenge ahead to get ready for. Joshua chapter 12 highlights a list of thirty-one kings defeated under his rule. Joshua didn't slow down to do touchdown dances; he had more work to do. "Therefore let us be grateful for receiving a kingdom that cannot be shaken, and thus let us offer to God acceptable worship, with reverence and awe" (Hebrews 12:28).

- Kneel: Recognition of the Father through prayer is not always the most popular stance in today's culture. Yet we see some athletes take a knee after a touchdown to thank God and give honor to their Savior. Tim Tebow may be the most recognizable yet scrutinized player for his devotion to God on the field. His act of taking a knee after touchdowns is made fun of yet doesn't stop his dedication. "Blessed are you when others revile you and persecute you and utter all kinds of evil against you falsely on my account. Rejoice and be glad, for your reward is great in heaven, for so they persecuted the prophets who were before you" (Matthew 5:11–12).

- Ickey Shuffle: Many players have their own style and creativity after they score a touchdown. In the 1980s, Cincinnati Bengal's running back Ickey Woods made famous an awkward shimmy back and forth known as the Ickey Shuffle. It's a move he'll always be remembered for and will remain in the hearts of the "Who Dey?" faithful. Some players have obnoxious dances while others are classy, but is this the identity you'd want to be remembered for by those who know you?

- The Lambeau Leap: Infamous Lambeau Field is the home of the Green Bay Packers, and the place Noah made his mark. It is also the place where NFL players leap into the stands to celebrate touchdowns with the fans. There are many famous places known for the celebrations of God's people. "When your children ask their fathers in times to come, 'What do these stones mean?' then you shall let your children know, 'Israel passed over this Jordan on dry ground'" (Joshua 4:21–22). Some places are set apart for remembrances and

memories. You can make good memories in your home,
marking it a place where Jesus is known as the priority.

Noah doesn't want to be known as the guy who had a good
year as a Packer or as the guy who missed out on a big
contract. "My identity was never going to be as a football
player. My identity is going to be in Christ and my name
will be in the book of life. It was a sobering moment, but
one I can look back and truly be thankful for," he said.

Don't let sports define you. It is a season of your life, but
not life itself. "In all your ways acknowledge him, and he
will make straight your paths" (Proverbs 3:6).

DAY 28

SURROUND YOURSELF WITH LIKE-MINDED PEOPLE

Ben Utecht
Super Bowl Champion Tight End
Indianapolis Colts

By Del Duduit

Fulfill my joy by being like-minded, having the same love, being of one accord, of one mind. Let nothing be done through selfish ambition or conceit, but in lowliness of mind let each esteem other better than himself.
—Philippians 2:2–3 NKJV

Ben Utecht knows about teamwork. He played for the Indianapolis Colts from 2004–2007 and for the Cincinnati Bengals from 2008–2009.

He chose to retire from the game after a series of concussions and head injuries.

But while he was with the Colts, the team won the Super Bowl. To be on a championship squad takes total teamwork and effort from all on the roster. There is no room for those who will not pull their weight.

When everyone works together, a team can accomplish great things.

The church is no different. A strong bond of fellowship among believers leads to a powerful body of Christ. This is necessary as new battles continue to rise up from the enemy.

"When you look through the lens of Christianity, you have to understand what you are up against," Ben said. "The game has changed, but as long as we have people like Benjamin Watson and Tony Dungy around us—guys who are willing to be a voice and a champion of faith—we will be okay."

He also pointed to men like Tim Tebow, who draws scrutiny from nonbelievers, yet he attracts thousands of people when he participates in an event. "He loves people, and that's why they flock to him," he said. "There is something about loving people that makes you want to get near them."

Perhaps this is why the late Billy Graham drew millions of people to his crusades. He showed love and total humility whenever he preached the Word of God.

Ben likes to be around others who share his spiritual beliefs. He said it just makes life easier if you hang with those who have similar convictions.

"It's important to trust in the Lord, but it's also important to surround yourself with fellow Christians," he said. "I grew up in a Christian home, and that was tremendous. But it was just as great when I played in Indianapolis to be around a bunch of guys who loved the Lord too."

There is a component of comradery that surrounds a solid team—just look at the Colts' championship rings, which have the word *faith* engraved on them. "To my knowledge, we have the only rings in history of the NFL to have a spiritual message, and that is cool," he added. "We had a great bunch of guys there."

> A man who has friends must himself be friendly, but there is a friend who sticks closer than a brother.
>
> —Proverbs 18:24 NKJV

In the Huddle

Who is in your inner circle of friends? Maybe you find yourself around the wrong crowd once in a while. This can happen easily. The devil doesn't want you to be a strong Christian, and he prefers you to be weak and relaxed in your spiritual walk. This is why he surrounds you with bad influences at work. You can have strong friendships with people who are not followers of the Lord. But in these cases, you need to be a guiding light and set a righteous example. Have the guys ever invited you out after work, and you know it is a bad idea to go because their plans are questionable? Did you go anyway? Remember how uncomfortable this made you feel, and be careful not to hinder your witness.

Cross the Goal Line

Not everyone is like Ben and has strong Christian friends like Benjamin Watson or Tony Dungy. But chances are you know some well-established men in your church or at work who would make good friends. Relationships with men of character will ground you, make you accountable, and strengthen you as a Christian. Here are some biblical reasons why you should use care when you select your friends:

- The right friend will not try to lead you away from the Lord: Instead, a true friend will encourage you to seek God to help you through life's challenges. "The righteous should choose his friends carefully, for the way of the wicked leads them astray" (Proverbs 12:26 NKJV). Do you want to pal around with a person who might compromise your convictions, or do you want someone who will help you to uphold them?

- The right friend will stand by you and provide counsel: Sometimes it's good to just talk to a friend about life's issues. A person you can place your complete confidence in is a treasure. A friend you can trust is worth more than gold. "Listen to counsel and receive instruction, that you may be wise in your latter days" (Proverbs 19:20 NKJV).

- The right friend will hold you accountable: If you begin to make some unusual decisions at work or socialize with a member of the opposite sex, a good colleague will point out the red flags that can lead to potential problems. A true friend will always be honest and tell you what you may not want to hear. But keep in mind, medicine often tastes bad on the way down, but it is needed to make you well. "As iron sharpens iron, so a man sharpens the countenance of his friend" (Proverbs 27:17 NKJV).

- The right friend will worship Christ and pray for you: What more could you ask for from a friend? When a fellow believer praises God with you and gets down on his knees on your behalf, count this a blessing. "A friend loves at all times, and a brother is born for adversity" (Proverbs 17:17 NKJV).

The right friend is also a person who will stay by your side through good and bad times. But most of all, he will stand up for what is right and won't give in to the pressures of the world. Money can't buy friendship. A good friend must be sought and prayed for, and once you find him, try to hang onto him. Make sure to select friends with whom you bear witness. This matters in life. You want your children to associate with other teens who have solid morals and values, so you should do the same. Surround yourself with honest and moral people.

DAY 29

JOURNAL FOR GOD'S GLORY

Morgan Cox
All Pro Long-Snapper and Super Bowl Champion
Baltimore Ravens

By Del Duduit

Therefore, my beloved, as you have always obeyed, not as in my presence only, but now much more in my absence, work out your own salvation with fear and trembling; for it is God who works in you both to will and to do for His good pleasure.

—Philippians 2:12–13 NKJV

Morgan Cox flings footballs back to kickers for a profession. He is an All-Pro long-snapper for the Baltimore Ravens and was part of the team that won Super Bowl XLVII.

He spends hours each day practicing his craft. Most NFL fans take what he does for granted. But if he makes a mistake, he gets everyone's attention. He role on the special teams is simple, yet highly important. His performance makes a tremendous impact on his team's field position. For this reason, he stays prepared and ready at all times.

Readiness was also a key focus when he and his wife found out a baby was on the way.

"It was a new challenge for us, so we wanted to do something special and prepare for our son," he said. "So, I did what my parents did for me."

The couple began to read the Bible together every day and make notes for their son Daniel to read when he became old enough. The couple wrote down lessons or takeaways from each Scripture and added what the verses meant to them.

Morgan's parents did the same for him his senior year of high school.

"What they did for me helped me to stay grounded in my faith," he said. "I had the idea to do this while Daniel was still in the womb."

He wanted to set a good example and later pass his beliefs down to his son.

"My goal is to be a man of God for him and let him see what's really important," he said. "I can be accountable to him, and keeping a journal helps me in that goal."

Morgan and his wife's intentions were to make sure their son know he was thought of before he entered the world. When he was born, they gave a wonderful gift to him—a strong heritage.

> Before I formed you in the womb I knew you; before you were born I sanctified you; I ordained you a prophet to the nations.
>
> —Jeremiah 1:5 NKJV

In the Huddle

Do you want to give a special gift to your children? Or do you want to make sure your life is captured in writing? Perhaps you desire a way to relive fond memories. A journal is a good way to do this, and it also helps you to express your innermost thoughts.

Cross the Goal Line

Morgan and his wife wanted to get a head start to present the gospel to him. There is no better time than today to begin. If you don't keep a journal now, you may regret it later. There are countless reasons to keep one, and here are some of them.

- Your life is on record: When you document what happens each day, there is a history of what you experienced.

- You can keep an account of God's providence: A written record allows you to revisit the times the Lord has poured down His mercy and grace on you and your family. Like the song says, "Count your blessings, name them one by one." At the same time, you can make notes about the times you struggled and then show proof of how God brought you through to victory. This may be an inspiration to you later when you read back over it or to your children in years to come.

- You can remember your prayer list: As you grow older, you might find it helpful to write prayer requests down, so you don't forget to pray for them. Make a list of prayer needs from your friends and loved ones, and refer to it each day when you spend quiet time with God.

- You can document when prayers are answered: Each time an item on your prayer list is answered, put a checkmark next to the entry in celebration and in recognition of God's answer to your prayer, and write a date next to it. Give God all the glory.

- You can put life events into perspective: Sometimes, when you take a moment to write down the details of a situation, you might see it in a different light. Put it on paper, step away for a few minutes and revisit. The circumstances may appear different to you, and God might show you a better way to handle the matter.

- You can practice your writing skills: This can be helpful if you have ever considered a ministry as an author. You may want to turn your journal into a book someday to help others.

- You can save it as a keepsake for your children: When you die someday, you can leave an example of how you lived your life for the Lord. Encourage your children to do the same to bless them and give them spiritual lessons for their future.

- You can keep your faith and story alive for years to come: If you leave your journal as a legacy to someone you love, then you can remain in their thoughts and prayers always.

- You can reinforce your relationship with the Lord: When you pen down your thoughts, prayers and desires, you can often strengthen your bond with Christ.

- You can leave a legacy: What better heritage to leave your children than written examples of how you lived for the Lord? "A good man leaves an inheritance to his children's children, but the wealth of the sinner is stored up for the righteous" (Proverbs 13:22 NKJV).

Consider the idea of starting a journal. If you have children, this can be a treasure they will keep forever. But better still, a record of your life can draw you closer to the Lord and help you to remain accountable to Him and to yourself. When you put down your thoughts and prayers, you make your requests known to the Savior. You can go into detail about how much He means to you and how much you love him. A journal can be wonderful therapy and a place you can call your own. This can also be a great way to commune with God one on one. If you haven't done so yet, begin your journal today.

DAY 30
STAY STRONG IN YOUR WALK

Anthony Muñoz
Hall of Fame Tackle
Cincinnati Bengals

By Del Duduit

Have I not commanded you? Be strong and courageous.
Do not be afraid; do not be discouraged, for the LORD your
God will be with you wherever you go.

—Joshua 1:9 NIV

When Anthony Muñoz entered the NFL in 1980, he didn't
know many of his fellow players.

Many experts viewed the first-round draft pick of the
Cincinnati Bengals from the University of Southern California as a risk. He had some knee problems and did not
play much the final two seasons of his college career due
to injuries. But he had an instant impact in the Queen
City and was a mainstay in the lineup for the next thirteen
seasons. Today he is considered by most experts to be the
greatest offensive lineman to have ever played the game.

He worked hard in practice and in the off-season and
remained loyal to the Lord through his daily devotions. He
became involved with like-minded ministries and stayed

active in church. But perhaps one of the best moves he made was to surround himself with good people.

"When I came to the NFL, I was a young Christian man," he said. "I felt like Gilligan on an island trying to stand strong and just survive."

But he quickly found men of similar character and spent time with them to help him along the way.

"It didn't take me long to find out who were followers of the Lord, and I hung out with them," he said. "We [he and his wife] joined a church in Cincinnati, and they helped us get established. That's important for all married couples."

Anthony said over his career, he saw his share of difficult times in the NFL locker room. The best way he found to overcome the challenges was to stay strong and hold to his convictions.

"The guys respect that, even if they don't agree," he said. "All of sudden when they see you walk the walk and talk the talk, they will honor and appreciate your stance."

He calls this lifestyle evangelism.

"If you don't back up what you say, then they pick up on that right away and make it tough for you," he said. "Just take a stance and hold firm, and don't condemn anyone."

When he played, Anthony estimated about 90 percent of his fellow players were nonbelievers. He viewed this as an opportunity to witness to his teammates every day.

"I wanted them to see a difference in me," he said. "I wanted them to see Christ in me, so that's how I lived."

His actions on and off the field spoke volumes.

He was the first member of the Bengals to be inducted into the NFL Hall of Fame. He won numerous awards, which included the 1991 NFL Man of the Year Award and the 2004 Walter Payton Award for outstanding civic involvement.

"When you give back, that's what God wants," he said. "But it all starts with having the right group of people around you."

> Whatever you do, work at it with all your heart, as working for the Lord, not for human masters.
> —Colossians 3:23 NIV

In the Huddle

Who do you associate with at work or in your personal life—Christians or nonbelievers? You are perfectly fine to spend time with those who do not profess faith, but be careful. Your friends and coworkers who don't follow Christ will watch how you handle situations to see if you practice what you preach. Don't let them place you in a compromising position.

Cross the Goal Line

Anthony surrounded himself with like-minded people in the locker room. The group may have been small, but the members carried a lot of weight. There are many benefits to Christian fellowship. Lifelong friendships are made, and alliances are formed. Good friends are a true blessing. This does not mean you should never socialize with nonbelievers, but try to spend the majority of your time with those who have similar morals and values. Here are some reasons why:

- Encouragement: When you invite Christian fellowship, you can enjoy the company of those who share your beliefs. You can laugh together and at the same time, you can help each other through difficult challenges. You cannot place a price on joy and happiness that comes through Christ. "One who has unreliable friends soon comes to ruin, but there is a friend who sticks closer than a brother" (Proverbs 18:24 NIV).

- Worship: When you praise the Lord in unison and share the loving grace of the Savior, you form a strong bond with lifelong friends. You are not limited to fellowship inside the church walls only. Worship together can also take place outside of the sanctuary in other scenarios such as home Bible studies or Sunday school class meetings. You might even lead your friends in devotions out on the golf course or on vacation. "Greater love has no one than this: to lay down one's life for one's friends" (John 15:13 NIV).

- Service to others: Get involved in church activities with a purpose to help the underprivileged in your neighborhood. Sing Christmas carols to shut-ins or visit members of the church who are in hospitals or nursing homes. Demonstrate compassion to those in need, and show Jesus to others by shining the light of Christ on your local community. "For where two or three gather in my name, there am I with them" (Matthew 18:20 NIV).

- Acceptance: Everyone longs to be welcomed into the fold. Anthony said when he first arrived in the league, he felt isolated—as though he were stranded on an island. Acceptance is one of the many benefits when you join a church. There you won't feel left out in the dark, but don't expect people to read your mind either. Talk to your pastor, tell him you want to be involved, and let him point you in the right direction.

• Family: You may have a wonderful family at home, but you need others in your life to help you along the way. In addition to his wife, Anthony also needed male colleagues who shared his philosophy. He gained strength because his friends held him accountable. Make a point to find people of like faith, and let them be of service. You can set an example for them too. Hold each other to a higher standard, and let them see you mean business about serving the Lord. "Walk with the wise and become wise, for a companion of fools suffers harm" (Proverbs 13:20 NIV).

Good Christian friends are hard to find. The best place to locate them is in your church. Take the initiative and become involved in activities, or start some yourself. When you partner with the right people, you can form you own All-Pro team and finish the season undefeated.

If you enjoyed this book, will you consider sharing the message with others?

Let us know your thoughts at info@ironstreammedia.com. You can also let the author know by visiting or sharing a photo of the cover on our social media pages or leaving a review at a retailer's site. All of it helps us get the message out!

Facebook.com/IronStreamMedia

———————

Iron Herring, Ascender Books, New Hope® Publishers, Iron Stream Books, and New Hope Kidz are imprints of Iron Stream Media, which derives its name from Proverbs 27:17, "As iron sharpens iron, so one person sharpens another."

This sharpening describes the process of discipleship, one to another. With this in mind, Iron Stream Media provides a variety of solutions for churches, ministry leaders, and nonprofits ranging from in-depth Bible study curriculum and Christian book publishing to custom publishing and consultative services. Through our popular Life Bible Study, Student Life Bible Study brands, and New Hope imprints, ISM provides web-based full-year and short-term Bible study teaching plans as well as printed devotionals, Bibles, and discipleship curriculum.

For more information on ISM and its imprints, please visit IronStreamMedia.com.

Find More from the NFL's Best in Volume 1

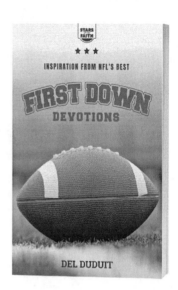

Inside this book, Del Duduit brings out obstacles faced by some of the most recognizable names in the National Football League. And how did they get through their trials? The same way I do. We let Christ fight our battles."

~ William White, retired NFL player

"For college football fans outside of the SEC, it is just a game. But, to the Tigers, the Iron Bowl is just as important as a National Championship. Del uses this long-standing rivalry to focus in on the battle in our faith where 'iron sharpens iron.' Read some of the great gridiron moments for Auburn while sharpening your faith for your own spiritual playbook." — Ben Cooper, author and speaker

AUBURN BELIEVER

40 DAYS OF DEVOTIONS FOR THE TIGER FAITHFUL

DEL DUDUIT

Calling all Tiger Faithful

"So much history, so much winning. Author Del Duduit does a brilliant job of sharing both. Southern pride in Christ and Alabama football can be found throughout this devotional. A must-read for all Crimson Tide fans and for all followers of Christ."
—Cary Knox, author, inspirational speaker, teacher, and coach

For the Roll Tide Faithful

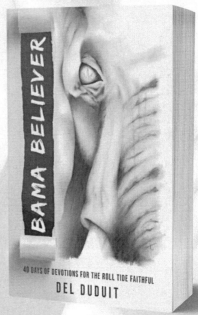

BAMA BELIEVER

40 DAYS OF DEVOTIONS FOR THE ROLL TIDE FAITHFUL
DEL DUDUIT

"Del Duduit has collected wonderful gems of faith from a variety of MLB's best players and coaches who are dedicated to bringing glory to Christ and shining their light for Him."
~ Blaine Boyer, MLB pitcher